Shalom:

A 60-Day Journey to All-Encompassing Peace

Shalom:

A 60-Day Journey to All-Encompassing Peace

Deborah Schaulis

Dedication

This book is dedicated to *Yahweh Shalom*, the God of peace; to Jesus Christ, who is our peace; and to the Holy Spirit, in whose presence is peace.

You have stilled the storms in my heart
    and taught me to rest in You.
Lord, no matter what I walk through,
    I know I am safe with You.

It's also dedicated to our faithful supporter and intercessor, Sarah Ricks. You carry peace wherever you go, sweet friend. May the Lord bless you for bringing tranquility and wisdom to so many souls!

Contents

Acknowledgments

Introduction   1

Day 1   Peaceful Passing   3

Day 2   Promised Peace   5

Day 3   Impediments to Peace   7

Day 4   Answer of Peace   9

Day 5   Released in Peace   11

Day 6   Peace and Harmony   13

Day 7   National Peace and Tranquility   15

Day 8   Peace in Yahweh's Name   17

Day 9   Yahweh Is Peace   19

Day 10   Peace in Agreement   21

Day 11   Covenant of Peace   23

Day 12   Peaceful Kingdom   25

Day 13   Peace Between Neighbors   27

Day 14   All Is Well   29

Day 15   No Peace with Witchcraft   31

Day 16   Peace to a Tender Heart   33

Day 17   Partnership of Peace   35

Day 18   Making Peace   37

Day 19   Man of Peace   39

Day 20   Peace or Adversity   41

Day 21	Peace and Truth	43
Day 22	Sleeping in Peace	45
Day 23	Peace Despite Insincerity	47
Day 24	Strength and Peace	49
Day 25	Seek Peace	51
Day 26	Our Peace Delights God	53
Day 27	Immeasurable Peace	55
Day 28	No Peace Where Sin Resides	57
Day 29	Rescued from Battle	59
Day 30	Peace and Prosperity to Come	61
Day 31	Peace Rather Than Folly	63
Day 32	Security of a Lawful Lifestyle	65
Day 33	Peace Among Warring Factions	67
Day 34	Peace for the City of Peace	69
Day 35	Peace and Provision	71
Day 36	Pathways of Peace	73
Day 37	Promoting Peace	75
Day 38	Peace with One's Enemies	77
Day 39	Reign of the Prince of Peace	79
Day 40	*Shalom* Squared	81
Day 41	Results of Right Living	83
Day 42	God of War and Peace	85
Day 43	Peace for the Righteous	87
Day 44	Messengers of Peace	89

Day 45	Our Penalty for His Peace	91
Day 46	Peace We Can Count On	93
Day 47	Joy and Peace for All Creation	95
Day 48	Removed from Calamity	97
Day 49	Paths That Don't Lead to Peace	99
Day 50	Ever-Flowing Peace	101
Day 51	False Comfort	103
Day 52	Peace in Exile	105
Day 53	God's Good Plans	107
Day 54	Restoring Health & Well-being	109
Day 55	Safe Pasture	111
Day 56	Peace Where God Is Present	113
Day 57	Peace That Strengthens	115
Day 58	Where Peace Dwells	117
Day 59	Justice, Truth and Peace	119
Day 60	Peaceable Kingdom	121
	Finding Peace with God	123
	About the Author	129

Acknowledgements

Thank you, J. R. Polhemus, for prophesying over my husband and me that we'd bring peace wherever we go. You were unaware of this writing project which was already underway at the time, but your words were an unexpected and wonderful affirmation of what the Lord had placed on my heart.

I am so grateful for the fabulous input from my beta readers: Cecelia Eaves-Walker, Ray and Patience Gifford, Sarah Ricks, Katelyn Gresli, Denny Strong, Heather Frykberg, and Kristy Funston. Thanks, as well, to the Fountain Hills Christian Writers group and everyone else who prayed for the completion of this project.

I want to highlight the music of Young Min You, which so frequently served as the soundtrack for this writing process. You don't know me from Adam, but your worship album elevated me into the presence of the Prince of Peace, soaring far above the chaos all around me! Thank you for making the download, *Mixed Worship Preview*, available for free online.

As always, thank you to my sweet husband for making space and time for me to write and encouraging me to stay on track with this book.

Introduction

The Hebrew word, *shalom*, is pregnant with meaning. Used 236 times in the Old Testament, it is most frequently interpreted as "peace," yet it means so much more. According to *Strong's Greek & Hebrew Dictionary*, the word was also translated in the *King James Version* as well, peaceably, welfare, prosperity, safe, salute, saluted, health, peaceable and with fourteen other words.

Its ancient Semitic root suggested completeness, fullness or wholeness. It was used as a greeting wishing someone peace, well-being, prosperity, safety and health. It incorporated contentment, favor, friendship, happiness, quiet, rest, soundness, tranquility and welfare.

This all-encompassing peace is lacking in our world today. Yet it's something we all desire and need. To gain a greater understanding of what *shalom* is and how it can be acquired, this daily devotional will highlight verses containing the word for the next two months. My hope and prayer is that, as you study the Scriptures, you'll grow closer to God and gain a deeper sense of this peace in the process.

Shalom, my friend! May the God of peace richly bless you in every sense of the word.

Day 1: Peaceful Passing

*"...you will go to your fathers in **peace**.
You will be buried at a good old age."*
(Genesis 15:15)

This is the hope of almost everybody on the planet. We want to live long and productive lives with as little drama as possible. We don't wish to die in war or struggle of some kind. Our dream is to be surrounded by loved ones, as we pass quietly from this life to the next. Not everyone has the opportunity to experience this idyllic end of life. Yet, the Lord promised this to Abraham because of his trust in Him.

Yahweh had asked a lot of this man. He called Abraham out of his homeland, far from his family to start a new life in a foreign country (Gen. 12:1). He promised an innumerable host of descendants to an individual whose wife was beyond child-bearing age and infertile (Gen. 11:30 & 15:2-5). And He promised that those descendants would inherit a land populated by ancient civilizations of giants and idolaters (v. 7). Although none of this made sense, Abraham put his faith in God and His promises (v. 6).

The key to ending well is to trust God no matter what. His first word to Abraham

3

involved leaving what was familiar to him and following the Lord to something new. God challenges each of us to do the same.

Step away from the idols and familiar sins in your life and allow God to lead you into a life of faith and freedom instead. Live as the Apostle Paul expressed in Philippians 3:13-14: *"Forgetting the things which are behind, and stretching forward to the things which are before, I press on toward the goal for the prize of the high calling of God in Christ Jesus."*

Dear Lord, I want my entire existence to be an expression of the peace that comes from living in fellowship with You. Please forgive me for past behaviors and associations that drew me away from Your presence and peace. Lead me into those actions and attitudes that will result in a long, satisfying life, instead.

4

Day 2: Promised Peace

*Jacob vowed... "If God will be with me,
and will keep me in this way that I go, and will
give me bread to eat, and clothing to put on,
so that I come again to my father's house in
peace, and Yahweh will be my God, then this
stone, which I have set up for a pillar, will be
God's house. Of all that you will give me
I will surely give a tenth to you."*
(Genesis 28:20-22)

Jacob was a scoundrel. Although his father Isaac was a follower of Yahweh like *his* father Abraham, Jacob was more self-reliant. He tricked his older brother out of his birthright, and then tricked his dad into blessing him instead of Esau. Now homeless and penniless, Jacob was on his way to his mother's family to wait out his brother's wrath.

With a rock for his pillow, Jacob fell asleep. God appeared to him and promised the same blessings He had given Abraham and Isaac. Then He added, *"I am with you, and will keep you, wherever you go, and will bring you again into this land. For I will not leave you, until I have done that which I have spoken of to you."* (Gen. 28:15)

Jacob vowed in response to God's promise: If, indeed, the Lord would be with him, guiding, providing and protecting him, then Jacob would serve Yahweh as his God. He would not only worship Him in that very spot, but Jacob promised to give one-tenth of his income, too.

In God's presence is the peace, prosperity and protection we long for. His faithfulness to His word is reason enough to trust and follow Him. But it also makes Him worthy of our adoration and sacrifice. Whatever we have comes from God, so He deserves all of it. Have you committed yourself to Him?

Lord, You have promised Your peace and presence to those who rely on You. Forgive me for trying to achieve my goals on my own. Help me depend on You and give You Your rightful place and portion in my life.

Day 3: Impediments to Peace

*Now Israel loved Joseph more than all his children, ...and he made him a coat of many colors. His brothers saw that their father loved him more than all his brothers, and they hated him, and couldn't speak **peaceably** to him.*
(Genesis 37:3-4)

Sibling rivalry has been part of the human condition since the first brothers, Cain and Abel. Every child wants to be the center of his or her parents' attention. Trouble arises when brothers and sisters become jealous of that attention and try to monopolize it.

Israel, whom we also know as Jacob, should have realized the danger of sibling rivalry, having experienced it with his twin, Esau. Yet, he set his children up for conflict by favoring one son over the others. Jacob hand-crafted a special robe for his second-to-the-youngest son and made his other sons feel less valuable. In doing so, he destroyed peace in his household. The older brothers' envy led to hatred; their hatred led to verbal abuse, and eventually they resorted to violence and betrayal.

So much unrest, or lack of peace, in our homes and society stems from feeling devalued. Parents favor one child over another—

often unwittingly. Certain classes or races seem to have advantages others cannot attain. We feel singled out for abuse or neglect, unloved and unappreciated. Consequently, we lash out at those around us.

That's why we must understand our value in our heavenly Father's eyes. John 3:16 says we're so valuable God gave His only Son to save us from eternal isolation. According to Psalms 27:10, though our own parents forsake us, God will take us in! With this in mind, we're less likely to react when others seem to ignore or reject us. We can live at peace and speak kindly, even to those who misuse us (Mat. 5:44).

Heavenly Father, thank You for loving me enough to sacrifice your own Son! Forgive me for envying and disrespecting others or for lashing out at those who do the same to me. Help me respond peaceably to everyone with whom I come in contact.

Day 4: Answer of Peace

> *Joseph answered Pharaoh, saying,*
> *"It isn't in me. God will give Pharaoh*
> *an answer of **peace**." (Genesis 41:16)*

Pharaoh, King of Egypt, had two disturbing dreams. He woke up remembering the dreams, but he did not understand what they meant. Sensing that they were important, the king summoned his wise men, yet none of them understood the dreams either. That's when the royal cupbearer remembered Joseph, a fellow prisoner where he'd been incarcerated, and told the monarch how he had accurately interpreted his dream two years before.

When Joseph appeared before Pharaoh, the king said, *"I have heard...that when you hear a dream you can interpret it"* (v. 15). Yet Joseph made it clear that he wasn't the one with the answers. Elohim—the God of the Hebrews— would put the king's troubled mind to rest.

When he listened to the king, Joseph was granted insight into what Yahweh had been trying to communicate through the symbolism of the two dreams. Not only did God provide the interpretation, but He also gave the young man the perfect plan in response to that revelation. When Pharaoh authorized Joseph to carry out this advice, the nation of Egypt and other people groups were able to survive the economic disaster the prophetic dreams foretold.

How often do we turn to human beings for wisdom when we are troubled by something we don't understand? When we're sick, we go to a medical doctor. When we're mentally or emotionally distressed, we turn to a psychologist. In matters concerning the law, we consult an attorney. And so on. Yet how often do we receive a truly sound, complete, perfect response that brings tranquility, rest and contentment to our souls? Only God can give us the best answer when we need understanding.

Father, You are the One who knows all things—present, past and future. You understand me and my circumstances better than any so-called "expert." Forgive me for running to others when I should be consulting You first. Please grant me the answer of peace that will bring quiet to my soul.

Day 5: Released in Peace

*Moses...returned to Jethro his father-in-law, and said to him, "Please let me go and return to my brothers who are in Egypt, and see whether they are still alive." Jethro said to Moses, "Go in **peace**."* (Exodus 4:18)

Moses made some poor choices and went from Pharaoh's palace to a tent in the wilderness of Midian. Instead of a prince of Egypt, he was a lowly shepherd. For forty years he lived in obscurity, until Yahweh appeared in a burning bush and commanded Moses to lead the descendants of Israel out of slavery in Egypt to the land of Canaan.

Being called, commissioned and authorized by God (Exo. 3:2-10), Moses could have just packed up his household and left. However, he loved and respected his wife's father and asked to return to his homeland to see how his family was doing. In the process, he gained not only his father-in-law's approval, but his blessing. Moses was released from the responsibility of caring for Jethro's sheep (v. 1), and he was given leave without resistance from his new family.

Many of us could learn a lesson from Moses. While it's true that we ultimately answer to no one but God, He has put us under the authority of others for a reason. How much better our missions can be when we have the assent and blessing of our families, employers, churches, and other leaders!

If we respectfully approach those we serve when the Lord calls us to something new, we may find ourselves with important allies in our next venture. By leaving on good terms with nothing hanging over our heads, we make the transition to our new assignment smoother and easier.

Lord, thank you for the family, friends and employer I presently have. I've learned so much from them and owe them a debt of gratitude. Please help me finish my current assignment well and treat these people with respect, so that they'll release me with their blessings when it's time to move on. Help me to be sensitive to Your Spirit, so I do that with love and grace.

Day 6: Peace and Harmony

*"If you will do this thing, and God commands you so, then you will be able to endure, and all these people also will go to their place in **peace**."* (Exodus 18:23)

You're probably familiar with the expression, "I bit off more than I can chew." It usually means we've taken on too much responsibility. That was the case with Moses. After leading the children of Israel to freedom, he found himself in charge of millions of men, women and children who had no idea of how to conduct themselves without the direction of their Egyptian taskmasters!

Moses' father-in-law Jethro was intrigued by the miracles Yahweh had performed for His people. He heard a full report from Moses, and then spent a day shadowing his son-in-law at his new job (Exo. 18:1 & 5-13). Jethro saw Moses act as lawgiver, counselor and judge for the entire nation of Israel. He warned that this was a sure recipe for burn-out—not only for Moses, but for the people he was trying to help, *"...for the thing is too heavy for you. You are not able to perform it yourself..."* (v. 18).

Jethro advised Moses to delegate his responsibilities. Teach everyone the Law of God, but put trustworthy men in charge. They could hear any lesser disputes between the Hebrews and leave the more challenging issues to Moses. That way, he and everyone under his authority could share the burden and be satisfied with the results.

Are you trying to carry a load that's too heavy for you, feeling overwhelmed and frustrated by all your responsibilities? How can you distribute the work, so you and those you're serving get along better? Jesus said His yoke is easy and light, and if we do things His way, we'll find rest for our souls (Mat. 11:28-30). Let Him provide a sensible solution!

Dear Lord, forgive me for taking on more than I can handle. Please show me how to manage my responsibilities better, so they're not so burdensome to me. Help me lead others well, so we can all go home satisfied each day.

Day 7: National Peace and Tranquility

*"I will give **peace** in the land, and you shall
lie down, and no one will make you afraid.
I will remove evil animals out of the land,
neither shall the sword go through your land."*
(Leviticus 26:6)

In Leviticus 26, Yahweh told His people
what benefits they could enjoy if they obeyed
the laws He handed down through His servant
Moses. Verses 1-2 highlight some of those national guidelines: *"You shall make for yourselves no idols...to bow down to it; for I am
Yahweh your God. You shall keep my Sab-
baths, and have reverence for my sanctuary...."* God wants us to keep Him first in our
lives, leave space for weekly times of rest and
reflection on Him, and participate in corporate
and individual worship.

In this verse, He offered *shalom* in all its dimensions—particularly peace, rest, safety and
general well-being—as an advantage of living
according to His instruction. Not only would
Israel be free from violence from within and
without, but they'd be safe from vicious animals. There would be nothing to threaten or
harm them, so long as they put God first and
followed His instructions!

Can you imagine living in a land free of conflict, danger or fear? That kind of utopia seems impossible in this day and age. But then, can we honestly say that our nation is living in accordance with God's Law? Unfortunately not.

That's why the Apostle Paul instructed us to pray for our leaders, *"...that we may lead a tranquil and quiet life in all godliness and reverence..."* (1 Tim. 2:1-4). He also admonished us to be good examples to those around us (Tit. 2:6-8). Domestic tranquility begins with the individual and spreads to those around him or her.

Father, thank You for Your promise of peace and safety to those who keep Your commandments. Please forgive me and my people for not keeping You first or obeying your Law. Deliver this land from that which threatens us from within and without. Help us to walk in reverence to You, so that we can enjoy Your favor and protection.

Day 8: Peace in Yahweh's Name

Yahweh bless you, and keep you.
Yahweh make his face to shine on you,
and be gracious to you.
Yahweh lift up his face toward you,
*and give you **peace**.* (Numbers 6:24-26)

When the Lord commissioned Aaron and his sons as priests, part of their responsibility was to invoke the name, or character, of Yahweh and His blessings upon the children of Israel (vv. 23 & 27). God wanted to bless His people, to protect them and lavish His kindness upon them, to demonstrate His love and favor. Yet He wanted those ordained as spokespersons to ask Him to grant those things.

Again, this wasn't just a lack of conflict God was talking about. It was the absence of all things bad and the presence of all that was good. He wanted His people to enjoy complete contentment, favor, friendship, health, happiness, productivity, prosperity, quiet, rest, tranquility and welfare. Those things were part of a packaged deal when they walked in the presence and fullness of God. When His character is reproduced in a people, those benefits come with it.

Are you proclaiming the name of Yahweh over yourself and your household, your workplace and your nation? Are you inviting His presence into every aspect of your daily life?

Remember, God doesn't just want to bless you, but to bless others *through* you!

1 Peter 2:9 says that believers are *"a chosen race, a royal priesthood, a holy nation, a people for God's own possession, that you may proclaim the excellence of him who called you out of darkness into his marvelous light."* It's our job to invoke the name of Jesus over everyone with whom we come in contact. When we do so, we'll begin to see His influence flow from our own lives to those around us.

Dear heavenly Father, thank You for Your kind affections toward those who represent You. Please set us apart for Your service, and help us to keep our eyes and those of others fixed on You. May Your presence, favor and peace rest upon us and those we love.

Day 9: Yahweh Is Peace

*Gideon said, "Alas,...I have seen Yahweh's angel face to face!" Yahweh said to him, "**Peace** be to you! Don't be afraid. You shall not die." Then Gideon built an altar there to Yahweh, and called it "Yahweh is **Peace**...."*
(Judges 6:22-24)

In Exodus 33:20, Yahweh warned that no man could see His face and live. The appearance of God's angelic messengers was so awe-inspiring, many Israelites trembled in fear when they encountered one of them, as well.

Such was the case with Gideon. At first, he thought he was talking to some holy man. But when the Angel of Yahweh performed a miracle, Gideon realized he was in the presence of someone greater and feared for his life.

The Lord reassured him, *"Shalom!"* The Holy Spirit whispered to Gideon's heart, much like a parent might quiet a frightened child, saying, "Hush, be still. There's nothing to be afraid of." God had no intention of slaying the man He'd called to deliver His people.

Gideon made a place of worship in that very spot. He called it *Yahweh Shalom*, or "I AM is peace." The writer of the book of Judges said it still stood in the city of Ophrah.

Do you have a personal place of worship—a quiet place where you can meet with the God of peace? In both the Old Testament and the New, we are told that God is holy and righteous and worthy of fear and trembling. Yet He loves us and has established a covenant of peace through Jesus Christ, so we need not live in fear of punishment (1 Joh. 4:15-19). It is from that place of reassurance you gain the courage to fulfill your calling of banishing evil and carrying the peace of God to others.

Yahweh Shalom, I want to walk in Your presence and Your peace. Please let me hear from You and know that You are with me to make me the mighty person of valor You have called and equipped me to be. May I walk in faith and confidence in You, and not in fear or doubt.

Day 10: Peace in Agreement

*Then Eli answered, "Go in **peace**; and may*
the God of Israel grant your petition
that you have asked of him." (1 Samuel 1:17)

Poor Hannah! She was childless in a society that considered her condition a curse or judgment from God. Her husband loved her and treated her with tenderness and deference, yet his other wife never let a day go by without rubbing Hannah's nose in the fact that she had children and Hannah did not. All the dear woman wanted was to give her husband a son.

When she went to the place of worship for the annual feast, Hannah was so despondent she couldn't even eat. She went alone to the tabernacle and poured out her heart to the Lord. When she couldn't voice the words, but only mouthed them, the priest thought she was drunk. Yet when she explained her tears were from grief and desperation, he blessed her instead. She was able to return to the family dinner and enjoy herself, confident God had heard her prayer and was going to grant her request.

In response to Hannah's prayer and Eli's blessing, Yahweh granted her not just the one son, but five other children (1 Sam. 1:20 &

2:20-21). Furthermore, the lad Samuel, whom she dedicated to God, became one of the greatest prophets Israel had ever seen. He helped to bring unity, peace and prosperity to the twelve tribes through his leadership.

Jesus was a great advocate of prayer. He said that when believers agreed together, not only would they receive what they asked for, but He would be in their midst (Mat. 18:19-20). God's favor is accessed when two or more approach Him with singleness of mind and purpose.

Father, You know the desires of my heart. You're aware of that one thing I long for more than any other. Unite my heart with Yours, so that I want what You want. Send me someone to agree with me in prayer, so together we can access Your grace and receive Your favor and peace in Jesus' name.

Day 11: Covenant of Peace

*Jonathan said to David, "Go in **peace**, because we have both sworn in Yahweh's name, saying, 'Yahweh is between me and you, and between my offspring and your offspring, forever.'"* (1 Samuel 20:42)

Jonathan was the embodiment of loyal love. From the moment David defied the giant Goliath, *"the soul of Jonathan was knit with the soul of David, and Jonathan loved him as his own soul"* (1 Sam. 18:1). The prince found in the valiant son of Jesse a true soul mate, in the purest sense of the word. Yet he also loved and respected his father, King Saul.

When David confided to his friend that Saul was trying to kill him, Jonathan could hardly believe it. Nevertheless, he promised to feel his father out for David's sake. He took a solemn vow to warn David, so he could live in peace and safety, even if it meant going against his dad. (1 Sam. 20:1-23)

When Jonathan learned of his father's intentions, it grieved him to see the king treat his friend so shamefully. He kept his appointment with David and sent him away for his own safety, weeping that it had to be so (vv. 24-41). As they parted, the two young men pledged their allegiance to each other and promised to be kind to one another's family, no matter what happened. Both David and Jonathan were true to their word.

Is there a Jonathan in your life? Do you have someone with whom your heart has been knit, *"a friend who sticks closer than a brother"* (Pro. 18:24)?

Jesus' love for us is even more perfect than what existed between David and Jonathan. He laid down His life to save yours, and through His sacrifice established an eternal covenant of peace that can't be broken. When we walk in agreement with Him, we know we can enjoy perfect friendship and safety.

Dear Jesus, thank You for loving me enough to give Your life for me. Thank you for being my truest Friend. Help me to walk in that same loyal love and peace with God and men.

Day 12: Peaceful Kingdom

*For he had dominion over all the region
west of the Euphrates.... And he had **peace**
on all sides around him. And Judah and Israel
lived in safety...every man under his vine
and under his fig tree, all the days of Solomon.*
(1 Kings 4:24-25, ESV)

When Solomon ruled over Israel, peace and prosperity abounded. In fact, the very name, Solomon, means "peace." The nation of Israel grew to its largest extent under King Solomon's reign, and monarchs from all over the world came to pay their respects because of the extraordinary wisdom God granted the king. Not only did the children of Israel live in safety, but those kingdoms under Solomon's authority enjoyed the same. They were blessed as Israel was blessed.

That phrase about every man dwelling under his vine and fig tree is particularly lovely. According to Micah 4:2-4, that is an expression of the ultimate in security and well-being— when people are able to concentrate on living useful, productive lives, rather than concerning themselves with warfare. It's a time of equity and security, when everyone gets to enjoy the fruits of their labors, and no one goes without food or shelter.

Wouldn't it be wonderful to experience that kind of peace, security and well-being? Why don't we? Partly because we don't have leaders running our nations, states, provinces, counties, parishes and cities by the wisdom of God.

According to James 3:13-18, peace is the fruit of godly wisdom; whereas conflict arises when men and women operate under worldly wisdom. When a nation is governed by individuals driven by the jealousy and selfish ambition that characterize the so-called wisdom of demons or men, *"confusion and every evil deed"* result. That's why it's so important to pray for the wisdom we and those in authority need to live well.

Father, thank You for Your perfect wisdom. Please empty me of any thoughts that do not have their origin in You. Help me and my countrymen walk in heavenly wisdom, so that we can enjoy the fruit of our labors in perfect peace and security for all.

Day 13: Peace Between Neighbors

*"Yahweh gave Solomon wisdom, as he promised him. There was **peace** between Hiram and Solomon, and the two of them made a treaty together."* (1 Kings 5:12)

1 Kings 3:5-12 tells of a divine encounter in which Yahweh appeared to King Solomon in a dream and asked what the young monarch wanted. In answer to his request, God not only gave Solomon understanding and discernment to lead his own subjects well, but to deal right-eously with leaders of other nations.

When Hiram, king of Tyre, paid his respects to Solomon after he succeeded his father David, Solomon reminded his father's friend of King David's wish to build a temple for Yahweh, the God of Israel. He asked Hiram to provide building supplies and skilled laborers to con-struct it. At Hiram's request, Solomon supplied the neighboring kingdom with agricultural goods produced in Israel. In this climate of mutual respect and commerce, the two kings formed an alliance that lasted for quite some time and brought blessings to both dominions.

Peace is possible, when nations and king-doms adopt an attitude of cooperation, rather than domination. When one country trades equally with another, acknowledging the sovereignty and dignity of the other, then foreign relations go well. But when one people group assumes that they are better than another, or one desires what the other has but is unwilling to trade equitably with them, then conflict arises.

This is true with individuals as well as with nations. Followers of Christ are commanded to do our best to *"be at peace with all men"* (Rom. 12:18). This godly respect and congeniality are reflections of the character of Christ, our *"Prince of Peace"* (Isa. 9:6). By loving our neighbors as we love ourselves, we can enjoy peaceable relationships free from division and strife (Gal. 5:13-15).

Heavenly Father, You are a God who loves peace. Please help me to treat others with respect, so that we can live together in harmony. Help me to choose my friends wisely, so that I can enjoy good, healthy relationships. Make me the kind of friend others are happy to know.

Day 14: All Is Well

"Please run now to meet her, and ask her,
*'Is it **well** with you? Is it **well** with your*
*husband? Is it **well** with your child?'"*
*She answered, "It is **well**." (2 Kings 4:26)*

Elisha the prophet found a wonderful bene-factor in the city of Shunem (which means "double resting place"): a well-to-do woman, who opened her home to him. She even had a special apartment constructed, where he could stay whenever he passed through. Grateful for her hospitality, Elisha asked God to give her a son. (2 Kin. 4:8-17)

However, one day something terrible hap-pened. Complaining of a headache, the lad was carried from his father's field to his mother. He died in her lap (vv. 18-20).

Not mentioning this to anyone, the Shu-nammite laid the boy on Elisha's bed and went to find the prophet, telling everyone all was well (vv. 21-24). Elisha sent his servant to in-quire, using the word *shalom* three times: *"Is it **peace** for you? Is it **peace** for your husband? Is it **peace** for the boy?"* (2 Kin. 4:26, LEB, emphasis added). All she answered was, *"Sha-lom,"* which could've meant "Peace," or "It is well."

The grieving woman said to Elisha, *"Did I ask you for a son, my lord? Didn't I say, 'Do not deceive me'?"* (v. 28). So the prophet hurried to her home and pleaded with the Lord to revive the dead boy. When he was restored, the appreciative mother fell at Elisha's feet. (vv. 29-37)

Sometimes we say all is well, when it really isn't. Perhaps we say it in faith, hoping it will be. Other times we say we're okay, when we don't want to be delayed or have people feel sorry for us. In either case, our *shalom* is found, not in our circumstance, but in the goodness of Yahweh our God and His plans for our lives.

Yahweh, You are the Source of life. You give and take as You please. Help me trust Your goodness, even when all does not seem well. Please surround me with Your peace and presence, when I need it most.

Day 15: No Peace with Witchcraft

*When Joram saw Jehu, he said, "Is it **peace**, Jehu?" He answered, "What **peace**, so long as the prostitution of your mother Jezebel and her witchcraft abound?"* (2 Kings 9:22)

After King Solomon turned from Yahweh to idols, the nation of Israel was split into two kingdoms. The southern kingdom served God, while the northern kingdom plunged deeper into the occult. The notorious Queen Jezebel murdered prophets of Yahweh and employed hundreds of priests of Baal and Asherah, instead. She used seduction, manipulation, intimidation and other means to control others—including her son, King Joram.

God appointed Jehu to take the throne and execute everyone under Jezebel's influence. When Joram asked if his captain came in peace, Jehu indicated peace was impossible while Jezebel's witchcraft reigned. The only way to restore it was to destroy her and put an end to her black arts.

Witchcraft, idolatry and the shedding of innocent blood are detestable in God's sight (Deu. 18:10-14 & 27:15; Pro. 6:16-19). Moreover, any kind of rebellion is the same as witchcraft in God's eyes, and stubbornness is as bad as idolatry (1 Sam. 15:23). By rejecting the Lord's direction and doing their own thing, men and women disqualify themselves as leaders, and they bring turmoil into their spheres of influence—whatever those may be.

Is there evidence of witchcraft in your home, workplace, school, city or nation? If so, what are you doing to stop it? The way to counteract any spirit of rebellion is to act in the opposite spirit: yield. As James 4:7 says, *"Submit yourselves therefore to God. Resist the devil, and he will flee from you"* (ESV). The more you choose to obey Yahweh, the more His presence and order can come in.

Oh God, Your ways are perfect. You know better than anyone how to establish order and bring rest to a place. Forgive our rebellion and stubbornness; deliver us from witchcraft. Take charge now. Help me submit to You and those You have placed in authority over me. Help me to be a servant leader, rather than trying to control others.

Day 16: Peace to a Tender Heart

"'[B]ecause your heart was tender,
and you humbled yourself before Yahweh,
when you heard what I spoke against
this place, and against its inhabitants...
and have torn your clothes, and wept before
me; I also have heard you,' says Yahweh.
'Therefore...you will be gathered to your grave
in **peace***. Your eyes will not see all the evil*
which I will bring on this place.'"
(2 Kings 22:19-20)

Josiah was the last good king of Judah in a long succession of descendants of King David. Raised by a priest, he wanted to restore the temple of Yahweh which had been neglected by his predecessors. When scrolls containing the Law of Moses were found and read, the king was mortified at the curses declared against Israel for not obeying God's Word. He consulted a prophetess of Yahweh, who confirmed the message of doom.

God saw the grief and distress this caused King Josiah, so He reassured him that he would not live to see the evil coming upon his nation. He'd die in peace before then.

Josiah enacted the most extensive reforms ever instigated in the nation of Israel. He tore down idols and places of worship. He got rid of all kinds of evil practitioners and paraphernalia. He cleansed the temple and reinstituted biblical worship. (2 Kin. 23:1-24) Second Kings 23:25 says,

> *There was no king like him before him,*
> *who turned to Yahweh with all his*
> *heart, and with all his soul, and with*
> *all his might...and there was none like*
> *him who arose after him.*

Yahweh responds to those with tender hearts willing to accept correction and learn from Him. As James 4:6 and 1 Peter 5:5 say, *"God resists the proud, but gives grace to the humble."* He uses them to accomplish the extraordinary.

Lord, it grieves me to see what our society has come to, compared to what it ought to be. Please forgive us for our sins. Help me to be one of the change-agents who brings about reform. Let me bring my corner of the world out of chaos and confusion into fellowship with You.

Day 17: Partnership of Peace

Then the Spirit came on Amasai, who was chief of the thirty, and he said, "We are yours, David, and on your side, you son of Jesse. ***Peace, peace*** *be to you, and* ***peace*** *be to your helpers; for your God helps you." Then David received them, and made them captains of the band.* (1 Chronicles 12:18)

In 1 Chronicles 12, we read how God built David's band of mighty men while he was trying to avoid King Saul's efforts to murder him (See also 1 Sam. 27:1-7). Amasai came with a group of defectors from Judah and Benjamin.

When they approached his stronghold, David went out to meet them. He said,

> *"If you have come* ***peaceably*** *to me to help me, my heart will be united with you; but if you have come to betray me to my adversaries, since there is no wrong in my hands, may the God of our fathers see this and rebuke it."* (1 Chr. 12:17)

Responding to David's cautious greeting, the Holy Spirit uttered a blessing through Amasai—proclaiming peace, safety, and well-being to David and all the people allied with him. Amasai and his companions knew Yahweh was with David and that King Saul's days were numbered. They wanted to join the man after God's heart and partner with him. So David welcomed the men and gave them prominent positions in his army, which became the greatest in the land.

Whom has God put upon your heart as a partner in building His kingdom? Is there a ministry the Lord is blessing that could use your support? You may be led to join a law enforcement, military, legal or political action group to oppose injustice. Or you may offer your time, talents and treasure to help an organization or an individual bring the gospel of peace to your region or beyond.

Lord Jesus, Yours is the mightiest army in heaven and earth! I want to partner with You and whomever You have chosen to bring Your kingdom to my neighborhood. Please show me where and how I can do that.

Day 18: Making Peace

*When the servants of Hadadezer saw that they were defeated by Israel, they made **peace** with David, and served him. The Syrians would not help the children of Ammon any more.* (1 Chronicles 19:19)

King David was friends with Nahash, the king of Ammon. He sent a delegation to express condolences to Hanun, Nahash's son, after the elder king died. However, Hanun misinterpreted his motives and disgraced David's envoys. Then he hired a neighboring army to fight with him against Israel. (1 Chr. 19:1-7)

Twice David's army fought and defeated Ammon and their allies from Syria. The second time, the Syrians asked for terms of peace and never joined forces with the Ammonites against Israel again. (vv. 8-19)

The Ammonites picked a fight with those who meant to be their friends. The Syrians joined a fight that wasn't theirs to begin with and were beaten soundly. When they realized their error, they made amends and refused to make the same mistake again.

Do you find yourself in the midst of a conflict you never should have been involved with?

Proverbs 26:17 says it makes as much sense to meddle in someone else's quarrel as it does to grab a strange dog by the ears! It's better to get along with others than to waste time, energy and resources in a conflict that should never have happened in the first place. As Jesus said, *"Blessed are the peacemakers, for they shall be called children of God"* (Mat. 5:9).

If you find yourself in the middle of a messy situation, ask God to show you how to make it right. Humble yourself and apologize for whatever you've done to offend, and then do your best not to participate in that kind of situation again.

Dear God, I don't want to have my peace or that of others disrupted because I've taken up someone's offense. Please guard my heart and help me make good choices. Help me to make peace with those I've wronged and stay out of quarrels I shouldn't take part in. Help me be a peacemaker, rather than a trouble-maker.

38

Day 19: Man of Peace

*"Behold, a son shall be born to you, who shall be a man of **peace**. I will give him rest from all his enemies all around; for his name shall be Solomon, and I will give **peace** and quietness to Israel in his days. He shall build a house for my name...."* (1 Chronicles 22:9-10)

King David wanted to build Yahweh a temple—a permanent house of worship in Jerusalem to replace the tabernacle Israel had moved from location to location since their wilderness wanderings. God was pleased with the king's desire, but said David was not the man for the job. He was a man of war and had shed too much blood in his lifetime (vv. 7-8).

Instead, David's son Solomon was appointed to construct the temple. David subdued Israel's enemies, so his heir didn't have to deal with the threat of war. Not only that, but Solomon—whose name means "peace"—was a studious man rather than a warrior. He had no bloodguilt from murder or battle to stain his hands or heart. As David observed in Psalms 24:3-4, *"He who has clean hands and a pure heart"* is the one allowed to approach our holy God.

Solomon did build a house for the Lord which stood for centuries, until invaders from Babylon tore it down. However, another Son of David—Jesus, the Prince of Peace—built an even greater, everlasting temple consisting of those who believe in Him (See Isaiah 9:6, Eph. 2:13-22, Heb. 3:6 & 1 Pet. 2:5).

Are you a man or woman of peace? Is your primary concern to honor God through things of beauty and worship? Ask Him to show you how you can invest your time, talents and resources in ways that bring Him glory, rather than pursuing conquests and achievements. These offerings please God and bring rest to your soul and others.

Dear Lord, thank You for making me part of Your eternal house through Jesus. Let me honor you in all I do. Please make me a person of peace who creates things that bring You pleasure and glory.

Day 20: Peace or Adversity

*"In those times there was no **peace** to him
who went out, nor to him who came in;
but great troubles were on all the inhabitants
of the lands."* (2 Chronicles 15:5)

Yahweh sent a prophet to King Asa telling the monarch He would be with the people as long as they sought Him (vv. 1-2). If they did what pleased the Lord, He'd give them strength and reward their efforts (v. 7).

In contrast, God reminded the king of the days of the judges when, *"Israel was without the true God, without a teaching priest, and without law"* (v. 3). The nation was in disarray and troubled *"with all adversity"* (v. 6). They had no *shalom*—no peace, security or safety—but suffered conflict from within and without, because the people didn't follow God. As Judges 17:6 & 21:25 say, *"Everyone did whatever he considered right"* (GW).

Encouraged by this message, Asa and his people tore down the idols in Judah. They made a covenant with God and executed anyone who refused to follow Him. Once they did so, Yahweh revealed Himself to them and *"gave them rest all around"* (2 Chr. 15:15).

There is no rest for those who do whatever they please. Peace is directly connected with our commitment to obey God. We take ourselves out from under His protective covering so long as we do our own thing. We place ourselves under His care when we fix our eyes on Him alone.

Are you experiencing God's peace? Or are you shattered, in conflict and facing all manner of trouble? What idols need to come down in your life for you to enjoy His presence, power and prosperity again? He will be with you while you are with Him.

Dear God, You are willing and able to give rest to those who seek and serve You. Let me experience Your peace. Align my heart with Yours and help me remove every impediment to intimacy with You. I don't want to do what I think is right. I want to desire and do what pleases You, instead.

Day 21: Peace and Truth

He sent letters to all the Jews...of the kingdom
*of Ahasuerus, with words of **peace** and*
truth, to confirm these days of Purim....
(Esther 9:30-31)

The peace, safety and security of the Jews
was threatened because of one man's pride,
selfish ambition and abuse of power. Haman
the Agagite subverted the truth, characterizing
the entire Hebrew population as rebels against
the king of Persia and followers of a strange
religion. Through this deception, he gained
permission to exterminate them throughout
the empire on a particular day determined by
casting lots.

God turned the tables on Haman and other
enemies of His people by exposing their diabol-
ical plot and authorizing the Jews to defend
themselves. After Mordecai was appointed in
Haman's place as second-in-command to King
Ahasuerus [Xerxes], he and Esther encouraged
their countrymen to annually commemorate
this event. They named it "Purim" after the lots
used by Haman to set the date to execute his
plan.

When Mordecai penned his letters, he probably not only wished his countrymen well, but

encouraged them to conduct themselves peaceably among other residents of the empire. The last thing they needed was for the king to decide Haman was right and do something to keep them in line—or worse! Even in a foreign land, God's people needed to love their neighbors and live according to His truth and righteousness.

Racial prejudice and hatred for others never ends well. God made all humanity from "one blood," descended from a single ancestor, and He desires a relationship with every one of us (Act. 17:26-27). To imagine that any people group is deserving of death because they are different from us is to miss the heart of the One who created mankind in His own image. He wants us to live in harmony and to love one another as He loved us (Eph. 5:1-2).

Creator of all mankind, thank you for safeguarding Your own against those who misuse their power. Show me how to join You in defending the helpless like Esther and Mordecai did. Help me celebrate every miracle You work on my behalf.

Day 22: Sleeping in Peace

*In **peace** I will both lay myself down
and sleep, for you, Yahweh alone,
make me live in safety.* (Psalms 4:8)

Psalm 4 is a wonderful expression of the peace that comes from trusting God. King David started out by asking God to listen and help him out. Then he expressed frustration with people who tried to cause him problems. He took comfort in the fact that *"Yahweh has set apart for himself him who is godly,"* and that He would heed his cry (v. 3).

The king reminded himself and others to fear God and avoid sin. He compared doing the right thing to offering a sacrifice in worship. Obedience expresses trust in the Lord. He asked God to show His kindness and *"let the light of your face shine on us"* (v. 6).

By the final two verses, David had gotten the assurance he needed. In verse 7 he wrote, *"You have put gladness in my heart."* And then he anticipated a good night's sleep, knowing Yahweh would keep him safe.

Many people today have trouble enjoying adequate rest. They are disturbed by external conflict and internal struggles. They're riddled with regrets and tormented by anxiety. They wonder whether it's realistic to expect anything good out of life.

The secret to *shalom*—true tranquility of soul and rest for your body—is to make sure you have a clear conscience. David's advice to those suffering insomnia? *"Search your own heart on your bed and be still"* (v. 4). It's a good idea to take inventory each night before you go to bed to be sure all is well between yourself, God and others.

As Paul wrote in Ephesians 4:26, *"'Be angry, and don't sin.' Don't let the sun go down on your wrath."* When we live a life in harmony with God and others, it's easy to rest at night.

Lord, I need your shalom *tonight. Please clear my mind and conscience of anything that's keeping me awake. Help me to live a life that honors You, so I can enjoy true rest.*

Day 23: Peace Despite Insincerity

Don't draw me away with the wicked,
*with the workers of iniquity who speak **peace***
with their neighbors, but mischief
is in their hearts. (Psalms 28:3)

You've probably heard the expression, "He speaks with a forked tongue." It's a reference to the serpent (Satan, according to Revelation 12:9), who deceived Adam and Eve, as recorded in Genesis 3. This describes a person who says one thing but means another.

That's exactly what David referred to in this psalm. He knew how easy it was to be deceived by those who pretend to be friendly, but actually plan to take advantage of someone else.

Not only did David not want to become the victim of this kind of trickery, but he didn't want to be associated with such people. He indicated that those who lie and do evil don't have any respect for Yahweh. They're looking for trouble. David asked God to give them what they deserved (vv. 4-5).

Do you know people who act like they wish you well, but actually have something evil in mind? How should you respond? Should you try to get back at them?

Just after admonishing believers to do their best to live at peace with everyone, the Apostle Paul wrote, *"Don't seek revenge yourselves, beloved, but give place to God's wrath. For it is written, 'Vengeance belongs to me; I will repay, says the Lord'"* (Rom. 12:19). He concluded the chapter by saying, *"Don't be overcome by evil, but overcome evil with good"* (v. 21).

When people speak peace while plotting wickedness, our best response is to be kind to them and leave it up to God to deal with their dishonesty. Then we will have a clear conscience and enjoy peace with God.

Heavenly Father, I need Your wisdom to recognize when someone is insincere. Help me to be respectful of You and others by only speaking truth to my neighbors. Help me respond in peace and kindness, even when I am wronged. I trust You to correct wrongdoers and pray that You will reveal Your righteous character, so they do good instead.

Day 24: Strength and Peace

Yahweh will give strength to his people.
Yahweh will bless his people with **peace**.
(Psalms 29:11)

This song of David urges the *"sons of God"* to give God the glory He rightly deserves (Psa. 29:1-2, LEB). It describes the awesome power of Yahweh.

The Lord's powerful voice thunders over the waters; it's full of majesty, breaking mighty cedar trees (vv. 3-5). It is accompanied by flashes of lightning and *"shakes the wilderness"* (vv. 7-8). It *"strips the forest bare"* (v. 9a).

Everything in Yahweh's temple proclaims His glory (9b). Not only did He preside over the Great Flood, but He *"sits as King forever"* (v. 10). His power and authority supersede anything known to mankind.

Considering the greatness of God, why look to anyone else to give us strength and make us secure? Nothing can resist His power. He is King over all. As Proverbs 21:1 says, even the hearts of rulers are subject to His direction. He commands the elements to save you from damaging storms, fires, etc.

Jesus demonstrated this power when He was on the earth. When a storm arose on the

Sea of Galilee, Jesus' friends were terrified. The Lord *"rebuked the wind, and said to the sea, 'Peace! Be still!' The wind ceased, and there was a great calm."* (Mark 4:39) Jesus wondered why they were so afraid and faithless; they marveled at His authority over the wind and sea (vv. 40-41).

To whom do you look to strengthen, provide for and protect you? Are you trusting politicians, military, law enforcement or others? Or is your confidence in the One with authority over both natural and human forces?

The blessing of all-encompassing peace belongs to those who give Him glory, who praise His mighty name. Not only that, but people who willingly subject themselves to His authority can expect His favor, friendship, prosperity, tranquility and general well-being.

Thank You, Lord, for Your presence, power, glory and protection. You, more than anyone else, deserve our praise and reverence, since You have power over everything. Help me walk in peace, enjoying the strength and security You provide.

Day 25: Seek Peace

Who...desires life, and loves many days,
that he may see good? Keep your tongue
from evil, and your lips from speaking lies.
Depart from evil, and do good.
*Seek **peace**, and pursue it.* (Psalms 34:12-14)

Psalm 34 describes how Yahweh cares for believers. Written while David was running from King Saul and sought refuge with a Philistine monarch, it not only celebrates how God ministers to those dependent on Him, but gives advice to whomever longs for the benefits of a relationship with Yahweh.

First, David invited others to join him in worshiping the Lord (vv. 1-3). Looking to God, he took his focus off of his terrifying circumstances during Saul's insane pursuit and found peace, instead (v. 4).

David cried to God, Yahweh heard, and *"saved him out of all his troubles"* (v. 6). Verse 7 assures, *"Yahweh's angel encamps around those who fear him, and delivers them."* Psalms 34:8 says, *"Oh taste and see that Yahweh is good. Blessed is the man who takes refuge in him."* Verses 9-10 promise, *"there is no lack"* for those who fear and seek the Lord.

As verses 12-14 suggest, the good life comes from avoiding evil, saying and doing what is right. If you desire *shalom* with all its well-being, you have to go after it. The way you go after peace is to pursue its source, Yahweh. Verse 15 tells us He is attentive to the righteous.

When we experience the death of a loved one, abandonment, betrayal or some other loss, *"Yahweh is near to those who have a broken heart, and saves those who have a crushed spirit"* (v. 18). Although the hardships a god-fearing person faces are many, *"Yahweh delivers him out of them all"* (v. 19). He protects us physically and spiritually. *"None of those who take refuge in him shall be condemned"* (v. 22).

Oh, Yahweh, You deserve our praise, because You so faithfully look after us and grant us peace in the midst of all of our troubles. Help me run to You first, so I receive the help, provision and protection I need.

Day 26: Our Peace Delights God

Let them shout for joy and be glad,
who delight in my vindication; and let them
say continually, "Yahweh is great, who
*delights in the **welfare** of his servant."*
(Psalms 35:27, LEB)

In this psalm David complained about people plotting against his life and appealed to God to take action. Worn out and helpless before his foes, the psalmist urged the Lord to arm Himself and contend on David's behalf with those who contended with him. (Psa. 35:1-3)

In this imprecatory prayer, David asked God to humiliate those who unjustly tried to harm him. Rather than seeking his own revenge, he wanted heaven's righteous Judge to sort everything out. (vv. 4-10 & 21-26)

These people weren't reacting to something David did wrong. He considered them friends and prayed for them when they were sick (vv. 11-16). Not only did they repay him evil for good, but they plotted against other peace-loving individuals, as well (v. 20).

In the midst of his struggle, David took comfort in Yahweh's character. He anticipated salvation, knowing God delivers the weak from the strong (vv. 3 & 10). He knew God was aware of his plight and appealed to His righteous character (vv. 22-24). Confident that his prayer would be answered, David promised worship from himself and his friends because of God's kindness (vv. 27-28).

Have you felt embattled by those who unjustly accuse and taunt you? Don't try to get back at them. Entrust your cause to the Lord. He desires your well-being. He wants to give you His peace in the midst of your struggle.

While you may be tempted to speak harshly to those who misuse you, take the high road. Jesus urged us, *"Love your enemies, do good to those who hate you, bless those who curse you, pray for those who mistreat you"* (Luk. 6:27-28). Your real enemy is the devil, not humans (Eph. 6:12).

Righteous Judge, I present my case to You. You know what the enemies of my soul are up to. Please fight for me. Do what's best for all concerned—even the ones who've hurt me!

Day 27: Immeasurable Peace

But the humble shall inherit the land,
and shall delight themselves
*in the abundance of **peace**.* (Psalms 37:11)

In this psalm, David contrasted the lot of those who do evil with those who trust God and do what is right. In the first verse, he counseled us not to get worked up about wrongdoers or envy them. Their plots and schemes won't profit in the long run (Psa. 37:7). Corrupt individuals will be cut off—wiped out without a trace (vv. 2, 9-10 & 34-36). Their own devices will be turned against them (vv. 12-15). They have no future (v. 38).

However, those who love God and do what pleases Him enjoy all sorts of benefits. They're guided, vindicated, protected, provided for, satisfied and preserved by Him.

Verse 4 is my favorite promise in the Bible: *"Also delight yourself in Yahweh, and he will give you the desires of your heart."* The *Lexham English Bible* puts the first phrase this way: *"Take pleasure in Yahweh..."* It adds in verse 5, *"Commit to Yahweh your way; Trust also on him and he will act."* When we focus on God and what He wants, our desires align with

His. He grants the dearest things to our hearts and takes care of every concern.

The Hebrew word translated in verse 11 as "abundance" was first used in Genesis 16:10 to talk about a multitude of descendants that couldn't be counted. That's how much peace, prosperity and security God wants to lavish on those who turn away from anger, worry and wrongdoing to practice what's right!

So stop pursuing wealth like the wicked, and be generous, instead (vv. 21 & 26). God's got an eternal inheritance for those who trust Him (vv. 9, 18, 22, 29 & 34). Follow the examples of those who walk uprightly, *"for there is a future for the man of **peace**"* (v. 37, emphasis added).

Father, thank You for the favor You show those who trust You. Please help me to enjoy You and share what You give me with others, so they can experience Your shalom, as well.

Day 28: No Peace Where Sin Resides

There is no soundness in my flesh because of your indignation, neither is there any **health** *in my bones because of my sin.* (Psalms 38:3)

This verse comes from a song that recognizes the connection between our bodies and souls. David realized his lack of *shalom*—translated in the *World English Bible* as "health," but in other versions as peace, strength or rest—was due to unconfessed sin.

David opened by praying, *"O Yahweh, do not rebuke me in your anger or chastise me in your wrath"* (Psa. 38:1, LEB). He realized his suffering was because of God's displeasure with his sin. He complained the weight of his guilt was too heavy to bear (v. 4). Then he compiled a list of troubling symptoms.

David described infected wounds, pains that doubled him over, a burning sensation in his midsection, faintness, bruising, heart palpitations and lack of strength (vv. 5-10). His physical weakness and pain were relentless (v. 17). His pain was also psychological—including grief, depression and despondency (vv. 6, 9 & 13). David felt isolated from friends and family (v. 11).

What is the remedy for a lack of peace, due to our wrongdoing? Confession. In the *Holy Bible: Easy-to-Read Version*, we read, *"Lord, I told you about the evil I have done. I am sorry for my sin"* (v. 18). David concluded the psalm by asking for Yahweh not to forsake or remain distant from him, but to hurry and help him against his adversaries (vv. 19-22).

Are you physically or psychologically troubled? It may be due to some unresolved offense between you and God. Our consciences know, even when we refuse to admit, that sin separates us from our Lord. The lack of peace in our hearts can manifest itself as a lack of health in our bodies. The way to restore our health and well-being is to confess the wrong we've done and get right with God.

Lord, I am sorry for the things I have said or done to displease You or to wrong others. Please forgive my sin and restore my health and tranquility.

Day 29: Rescued from Battle

...I will call on God. Yahweh will save me.
Evening, morning, and at noon, I will cry out
in distress. He will hear my voice. He has
*redeemed my soul in **peace** from the battle*
that was against me, although there are
many who oppose me. (Psalms 55:16-18)

We've all had days when it feels like everyone and everything is against us. King David
experienced more than most. In this psalm,
he complained about restlessness in his soul
from the oppression of the wicked (vv. 1-3).
His heart ached and he feared for his life (vv.
4-5). He wanted to run away and hide in the
desert where no one could find him (vv. 6-7).

David's enemies weren't fighting with
swords, spears and arrows. They'd targeted
him with malicious gossip, division and deceit
(vv. 9-11). Worst of all, the guilty party was
someone he knew and trusted—someone who
regularly accompanied him to the house of God
(vv. 12-14)!

Rather than protect himself or seek revenge, David relied on the Lord (vv. 15-17a).
Even before the conflict was over, he anticipated the peace of God, knowing He heard his
prayers and would take action (vv. 17b-19).

David counseled himself and others to cast their burdens on Yahweh, knowing He would sustain and support them. Our Lord will never allow the righteous to be shaken or overthrown (v. 22).

The offender, on the other hand, broke his covenant of peace with David and others (v. 20). *"His speech was smooth as butter, yet war was in his heart..."* (v. 21, ESV). The king knew the days of such men were numbered (v. 23).

When assailed by pointed words as sharp as arrows—especially when they're aimed by friends you thought had your back—don't give in to the impulse to run or retaliate. Take your troubles to God. He can keep you safe in the midst of the most painful conflict.

Dear Lord, You are my peace. You're my rock and fortress, my defender. Guard my heart and mind from offense. Diffuse my painful situation and bring about a positive resolution.

Day 30: Peace and Prosperity to Come

During his days the godly will flourish;
peace *will prevail as long as the moon*
remains in the sky. (Psalms 72:7, NET)

The chapter from which this verse is taken
begins with the words, *"A psalm of Solomon."*
Yet many scholars point to the final line, *"The
prayers of David the son of Jesse are ended"*
(v. 20, NKJV), and assert that it was composed
for Solomon at his inauguration (See 1 Kings 1).
Not only does it anticipate what God would
do through David's son, but it prophesied the
reign of the Messiah to come. It's both a prayer
and praise to Yahweh for the fulfillment of His
word in 2 Samuel 7:12-16.

David asked God to give justice and righteousness to his son, so the new king could
judge Yahweh's people well, saving the needy
and punishing oppressors (vv. 1-2, 4 & 12-
14). Verse 3 said the mountains would be a
source of *shalom*; the hills produce the fruit
of righteousness. Some Bible versions translate
that word as peace, while others say prosperity.
Either way, the blessing of God is connected
with the godliness of His people. Verses 5-6
connect the fear of Yahweh with life-giving
showers on the earth.

Solomon's reign was limited to his lifetime and a specific geographic area, yet in verses 7-8, David described an eternal reign of peace *"to the ends of the earth."* He foresaw nations from all over the world bowing and serving the coming King (vv. 9-11).

As devoted subjects pray for and bless this beloved Ruler, productivity and fruitfulness will abound (vv. 15-16). *"His name endures forever...as long as the sun. Men shall be blessed by him. All nations will call him blessed"* (v. 17). The end result is that God will be praised and glorified for His *"marvelous deeds"* in Christ (vv. 18-19).

Yahweh, peace is a by-product of a righteous administration. Thank You that all-encompassing prosperity is something we can look forward to when Jesus reigns upon the earth. Help us enjoy the same benefits here and now, as we live in a way that honors You.

Day 31: Peace Rather Than Folly

I will hear what God, Yahweh, will speak,
*because he will speak **peace** to his people,*
even his faithful ones, but let them not
return to folly. (Psalms 85:8, LEB)

This song by the sons of Korah talks about the restoration of land and fortune that comes to those who turn back to God (Psa. 85:1). Not only did Yahweh forgive, but He covered over the sins of the descendants of Jacob (v. 2). He diverted His anger from them, so Israel could hope for salvation, instead (vv. 3-4).

The psalmist pleaded with the Lord to show His lovingkindness and *"revive us again, that your people may rejoice"* (vv. 5-7). These verses and the one featured above show that repentance, revival and salvation are instigated by God. He promises favor and blessing to those who realign themselves with their Creator.

Verse nine says, *"Surely his salvation is near those who fear him, that glory may dwell in our land."* God saves, not for our sakes alone, but ultimately for His own. Those who observe the *shalom* His people enjoy may revere and serve Him, too. Mercy, truth, righteousness and peace characterize the land that honors God (vv. 10-11). Good things come to those who listen to and obey Him; the land at peace with God and men is productive (v. 12).

It's easy to forget God and fall into bad habits when things are going well for us. Moses warned about this in Deuteronomy 8:6-20. In verse 18, he admonished: *"...remember Yahweh your God, for it is he who gives you power to get wealth; that he may establish his covenant...."*

When the Lord brings us out of a time of struggle and discipline, then restores peace to us, the last thing we want to do is return to the folly that brought trouble in the first place. As Psalms 85:10 indicates, *shalom* embraces the righteous.

Lord, I want Your favor and the blessings that come with it. Turn my heart away from foolishness; help me walk uprightly in obedience to You instead, so I can enjoy Your perfect peace.

Day 32: Security of a Lawful Lifestyle

*Those who love your law have great **peace**.*
Nothing causes them to stumble.
(Psalms 119:165)

This verse comes from the longest poem in the Hebrew psalter. Psalm 119 is an acrostic which celebrates God's Word. Instead of one verse that begins with each different letter, there are eight verses apiece for the twenty-two letters of the Hebrew alphabet. Of the resulting 176 verses, this is near the end in the section for "sin and shin," the twenty-first letter.

The first verse in the set says, *"Princes have persecuted me without a cause, but my heart stands in awe of your words"* (Psa. 119:161). The psalmist was more impressed with the wisdom of God than the threats of men. In verse 162, he rejoiced over the Word of God like someone who has found a tremendous amount of plunder. In contrast to falsehood, he loved the Law, and he praised the Lord for His *"righteous ordinances"* (vv. 163-164).

Those who love the Lord's decrees keep them. As verse 167 says, *"My soul has observed your testimonies...."* The next verse tells us the psalmist obeyed them, too.

The laws of Yahweh were written to help us live well. Therefore, it makes sense that we would feel a sense of security and well-being when we keep His commandments. There's no fear of punishment from God or men when we live the way we ought to (Rom. 13:3-5). We're less likely to fall into sin or the trouble it brings when we live according to our Manufacturer's instructions.

Psalms 119:166 says, *"I have hoped for your salvation, Yahweh. I have done your commandments."* When there is no offense between us and God, we can be confident He'll come to our rescue. That sense of well-being despite external circumstance is a comfort to those undergoing trials.

Have you experienced this kind of peace? Those who study and live according to God's Word are sure to find it!

Dear Lord, thank You for spelling out Your expectations for right living. Please help me learn and keep Your Word, so I can walk in safety and security.

Day 33: Peace Among Warring Factions

*My soul has had her dwelling too long
with him who hates **peace**. I am for **peace**,
but when I speak, they are for war.*
(Psalms 120:6-7)

This anonymously composed "Song of Ascents" is brief and to the point. Meant to be sung by worshippers going up Mount Zion to the temple, it tells how God previously answered the psalmist when he cried out to Yahweh in the midst of his distress (Psa. 120:1). Then the rest of the song voices his complaint and pleads for God's help this time, as well.

In verse 2, we read, *"Deliver my soul, Yahweh, from lying lips...."* Then the author warned of the consequences for those who deceive—including *"Sharp arrows of the mighty, with coals of juniper"* (vv. 3-4). We might say today that he "called down fire and brimstone" on those trying to bait him into trouble.

Next the psalmist complained about his neighbors: *"Woe is me, that I live in Meshech, that I dwell among the tents of Kedar!"* (v. 5). Meshech, which means "drawing out"—refers to descendants of Noah through Shem and Japheth. It's one of the people groups located north and east of Israel referred to in Ezekiel 38-39 as part of the kingdom of Gog, an aggressor who'll oppose Israel before Messiah returns. Kedar, which means "dark," was a descendant of Ishmael, a long-time troublemaker for God's chosen people. Those are the war-mongering people referred to in the final two verses of Psalm 120.

It's hard to get along with people when all they want to do is fight, especially when you are exiled in their land like the people of Judah were. Nevertheless, God is able to bring peace —even in the most difficult circumstances— when we fix our eyes on Him.

Father, You are the source of my peace and tranquility in the midst of conflict. Help me to be a person of peace, even when others are contentious. Help me carry Your nature and character into every tense situation and be the glue that draws people together instead of tearing them apart.

Day 34: Peace for the City of Peace

*Pray for the **peace** of Jerusalem.*
Those who love you will prosper.
***Peace** be within your walls,*
and prosperity within your palaces.
For my brothers' and companions' sakes,
*I will now say, "**Peace** be within you."*
(Psalms 122:6-8)

Another "Song of Ascents," Psalm 122 is attributed to King David. In verse one he began, *"I was glad when they said to me, 'Let's go to Yahweh's house!'"* This "man after God's heart," was excited about worshiping Yahweh (See Acts 13:22). He wasn't content with going someplace outside his city. He brought the worship center to the nation's capital, where his palace was located. That's why Jerusalem was highlighted in this song.

In verse two the psalmist set the scene: He was standing within the gates of the holy city. He noted it was densely populated (v. 3). It was the place where the tribes of Israel would go, as their God commanded, *"to give thanks to Yahweh's name"* (v. 4). It was also the seat of judgment for the king and his descendants (v. 5).

The name, Jerusalem, is Hebrew for "foundation of peace." So it is fitting we should pray for it to live up to the meaning of that name. David said those who love the city where God dwelt would prosper. He wished peace to everyone in it and prosperity to the royal palace. He understood that, when the nation's capital was at peace, Israel and all its inhabitants would benefit, as well.

Do you pray for the peace of Jerusalem? God promises blessings for those who do. What about your own government—whether local, regional or national? What would happen if you prayed for their peace? How might this benefit you and your compatriots? We should also pray for the leaders of our churches, so they enjoy their ministry and everyone can profit by it (1 Ths. 5:12-13 & Heb. 13:17).

Dear Lord, You know the condition of our nation. Our leadership is in turmoil. Please cause Your shalom to descend upon our civil and spiritual authorities, so we can all enjoy peace and prosperity together.

Day 35: Peace and Provision

*He makes **peace** in your borders.*
He fills you with the finest of the wheat.
(Psalms 147:14)

Psalm 147 is another anonymous song in the Hebrew hymnal. Verse two says, *"Yahweh builds up Jerusalem. He gathers together the outcasts of Israel."* God has counted and named every star (v. 4). *"Great is our Lord, and mighty in power. His understanding is infinite"* (v. 5). He heals the broken and wounded, supports the humble and defeats the wicked (vv. 3 & 6).

Praise and thanksgiving are fitting responses to this One who *"covers the sky with clouds,"* bringing rain to water the grass and feeding both domestic and wild animals (vv. 7-9). Yahweh isn't impressed by the strength of man or beast, but *"takes pleasure in those who fear"* and hope in Him (vv. 10-11). The Lord commands inclement weather, too (vv. 15-18).

Verse 13 acknowledges God's influence in maintaining the security of Jerusalem and blessing the children who live there. He is responsible for bringing stability and abundance to the rest of the nation, as well. As verse 14 pointed out, He didn't just give them the bare minimum required, but blessed their crops so His people were *filled* and satisfied with the *finest* and best food available! The closing verses celebrate how uniquely God related to the people of Israel by communicating with them and providing laws to govern them (vv. 19-20).

A nation's sustenance is closely tied to its security. Where there is war, you find famine (Rev. 6:1-6). Where there is peace, there is plenty—especially for those who fear and serve God.

When we rely on ourselves, we may do well enough. But, as Leviticus 26:3-12 and Deuteronomy 28:1-13 promise, those who look to Yahweh and do as He says enjoy the very best He has to offer.

Lord Almighty, You command the elements. Bless this nation with peace and provision. Secure our borders. Nurture our crops and livestock. Keep Your children healthy and happy. Thank You for all You have given and are going to give. Help us acknowledge Your kindness every day.

Day 36: Pathways of Peace

Happy is the man who finds wisdom....
Her ways are ways of pleasantness.
*All her paths are **peace**.* (Proverbs 3:13 & 17)

Asked in a dream what he most wanted from God, young King Solomon requested understanding to "*discern between good and evil*" (1 Kin. 3:9 & 2 Chr. 1:10). Yahweh was so pleased with this answer that He not only made Solomon the wisest man of his time, before or after, but He also granted the King of Israel more riches and honor than any of his contemporaries (See 1 Kin. 3:11-12 & 9:22). His fame spread so much, "*People of all nations came to hear the wisdom of Solomon...*" (1 Kin. 4:34).

During his lifetime, King Solomon coined 3,000 "*wise sayings*" (1 Kin. 4:32, NCV). In the book of Proverbs, he had a lot to say to his children and other readers about wisdom—which he frequently personified as a woman.

Proverbs 3:13-18 is a good example. The king noted how happy it can make a person to find and keep wisdom and the understanding that accompanies it (vv. 13 & 18). It is more profitable than precious metals or gemstones; nothing is more valuable in comparison (vv. 14-

15). Wisdom leads to a long and pleasant life, filled with riches and honor (vv. 16-17).

Wise people work hard and live frugally; they don't squander resources and can therefore enjoy financial security (Pro. 10:5 & 21: 20). The wise avoid evil, so they don't live in fear of harm (Pro. 2:10-22, 13:14, 14:16, 15:24, 28:7). They conduct themselves in a way that avoids unnecessary conflict, resulting in relational harmony (Pro. 11:12, 14:1, 24:3, 15:20, 16:14, 29:8 & 11). Wisdom can even help a ruler maintain national security (Pro. 20:18, 24:6).

God is the source of all wisdom. Seek His wisdom and then live by it. A life of physical, relational, emotional and financial well-being will follow.

Father, I want to experience peace in every area of my life. Please help me to live wisely, so I can enjoy that tranquility at home and wherever else I go.

Day 37: Promoting Peace

*Deceit is in the heart of those who plot evil,
but joy comes to the promoters of **peace**.*
(Proverbs 12:20)

Have you ever noticed how some people leave a string of confusion and conflict wherever they go, while others bring peace and harmony? Some folks seem bound and determined to take what others say the wrong way. They're constantly offended or offending someone else.

Others are actually amused by stirring up dissention. They prick and jab with pointed comments. They gossip, slander and pit people against one another. Before you know it, the whole home, office, church or classroom is in turmoil, and everyone but the troublemaker is miserable!

In contrast, there are those skilled at diffusing anger. They help people see things from each other's perspectives. These individuals encourage empathy and forgiveness. They bring their colleagues to consensus, rather than conflict.

In Matthew 5:9, Jesus said, *"Blessed are the peacemakers...."* The Greek word translated "blessed" in many English Bibles can also mean "happy." The word translated "peacemaker" is a compound of one verb that means "to make" plus another meaning "to join." So our Lord was saying those who work to bring people together are happy. This is similar to Solomon's statement in the second half of Proverbs 12:20.

Which kind of person are you? Do you come into a situation with a hidden agenda that soon has everyone at each other's throats? Or are you the one smoothing ruffled feathers and helping them get along?

If you're in the first category, you may be believing a lie from the enemy regarding yourself or others. There may be a spirit of rejection causing you to mistrust people and expect the worst from them—which is why you are easily offended or feel misunderstood. You need the God of peace to bring truth and a sense of well-being into your heart instead.

Father, forgive me for times I have been part of the problem instead of the solution in tense environments. Please let Your truth and peace reign in my heart, so I can carry it joyfully everywhere I go.

Day 38: Peace with One's Enemies

*When a person's ways are pleasing to the LORD, he makes even his enemies to be at **peace** with him.* (Proverbs 16:7, GW)

It's marvelous to be in the center of God's will; everything goes so much better! King Solomon said whoever lives in a way that pleases God enjoys freedom from conflict, because Yahweh pacifies his enemies.

This doesn't say a godly individual won't have enemies. As long as evil exists in this world, there will always be those who despise the just—simply because Satan hates God and whoever belongs to Him.

Those who resent god-fearing people may rant and rave against them, but they are limited in what they can do. Therefore, good men and women can live in security, despite the animosity of others. As King David wrote, *"You prepare a table before me in the presence of my enemies..."* (Psa. 23:5).

As we learned from 1 Chronicles 22:9-10, King David was assured his son would be a man of peace, whom the Lord would give rest from all his enemies. God promised to give the nation of Israel peace and tranquility during his administration. And that's what happened—at least so long as Solomon did what pleased Yahweh.

However, once he stepped from the safe confines of God's will, trouble brewed. First Kings 11 tells us that, after Solomon's foreign wives led him into idolatry, Yahweh grew angry with the king. Verse 23 says, *"God raised up an adversary to him, Rezon the son of Eliada...."* Hadad (a member of the royal family of Edom) and Jeroboam son of Nebat (who later established a separatist kingdom in northern Israel) also harassed King Solomon and his successors. Yet when godly kings ruled, the kingdom was kept safe.

Do you desire peace and safety from those who hate you? Then live in accordance with God's Law, and He'll look after you.

Lord, help me live in a way that pleases You, so I can enjoy the safety of Your care. Redirect Your servant whenever I start to stray from a lifestyle of obedience and peace.

Day 39: Reign of the Prince of Peace

For unto us a Child is born,
Unto us a Son is given;
And the government will be
upon His shoulder.
And His name will be called
Wonderful, Counselor, Mighty God,
*Everlasting Father, Prince of **Peace**.*
*Of the increase of His government and **peace***
There will be no end,
Upon the throne of David
and over His kingdom,
To order it and establish it
with judgment and justice
From that time forward, even forever.
The zeal of the LORD of hosts
will perform this. (Isaiah 9:6-7, NKJV)

Often quoted around Christmas time, this passage comes from a messianic prophecy partially fulfilled at Jesus' birth. As foretold by Isaiah 9:6, the Son of God was born to a virgin in the line of David's son, Nathan, and then adopted ("given") by Joseph from the royal line of Solomon (Luk. 1:35 & Joh. 3:16).

However the part about Him establishing peace, justice and equity has yet to be fulfilled. Jesus' first mission was to make peace with

God possible through the atonement. His reign upon earth will not occur until Christ's return and rule from King David's throne over the millennial kingdom (Rev. 20:4).

Jesus is the embodiment of God's character and nature. He's wonderful—extraordinary, without equal. He's a wise Counselor with the perfect plan to establish order. He is God incarnate with divine power.

He's everlasting—Jesus co-existed with the heavenly Father from the beginning. Having died and risen from the grave, He'll never pass away, but will live and reign forever.

As Son of the "God of peace" (Rom. 15:33 & 16:20, Php. 4:9, 1 Ths. 5:23), He is "Prince of Peace," able to bring worldwide harmony as foretold by the angels at His birth (Luk. 2:14). Unlike fallible humans, Jesus Christ will reign with perfect justice and righteousness—all with the backing of *Yahweh Tsabaoth*—the Lord of heaven's armies.

Lord, I know You are coming back to establish peace on earth. But I want to experience Your royal reign now. Align my will with Your perfect leadership. Help me live according to Your wise counsel.

Day 40: Shalom Squared

*You keep him in **perfect peace** whose mind is
stayed on you, because he trusts in you.*
(Isaiah 26:3, ESV)

This powerful verse isn't talking about just
any old peace, but all-encompassing peace.
Remember, one meaning of *shalom* is complete
or perfect. That's why we have the phrase "perfect peace" in this English translation, because
Isaiah used *shalom* twice in a row to emphasize
the magnitude of peace he was talking about.
Yahweh keeps in *shalom shalom* the person
whose mind is fixed on Him, trusting in Him!

Isaiah 26 follows a chapter that foretold
how Jesus would take away sin. That's why the
prophet celebrated salvation and said we could
enjoy peace. He assured his people that God
was a solid rock they could trust in, while those
who rely on the height of their cities for protection would be brought low (vv. 4-5).

In verses 8-9, Isaiah said Yahweh's judgments teach people to behave rightly. Yahweh
displays His majesty when He destroys those
who oppose His people (vv. 10-11). Using the
word *shalom* again, verse 12 says, *"Yahweh,
you will ordain **peace** for us, for you have
also done all our work for us"* (emphasis

added). He was responsible for increasing the nation of Israel and enlarging her borders (v. 15). When we cry out to Him in desperation, He comes to punish the wicked and rescue the weak (vv. 16-21).

Are you enjoying this peace of God? If not, it may be a case of misplaced trust. If you are relying upon anyone other than Yahweh and His Anointed, Jesus, to rescue and keep you safe and secure, that's probably why your sense of *shalom* is lacking. No person, weapon, wealth, institution or government can save and deliver like God! Stop trusting in human ability or resources. Depend on God alone to look after you. He'll do the work and you'll enjoy rest in your soul.

Father, forgive me for depending on myself or others to keep me safe. Give me the confidence that comes from trusting You alone to provide perfect peace, prosperity and protection.

Day 41: Results of Right Living

*The work of righteousness will be **peace**; and the effect of righteousness, quietness and confidence forever. My people will live in a **peaceful** habitation, in safe dwellings, and in quiet resting places.* (Isaiah 32:17-18)

How much does a person's lifestyle affect their health and well-being? Do people living rightly enjoy more rest and peace of mind?

Modern medicine and psychology recognize the correlation between our consciences and physical health. When we're anxious or stressed, it manifests in high blood pressure, insomnia, poor digestion, and a host of other issues. Whereas the person who has done nothing wrong sleeps well at night and is energetic and confident. We get a lot more done, too!

This passage shows that right living brings about mental and emotional tranquility—what we call "inner peace." But it also results in external peace.

Isaiah 32:15-16 connects domestic tranquility and productivity with an outpouring of the Holy Spirit. Desert areas become orchards, while orchards become forests; justice and righteousness are found in both.

As the Apostle Paul wrote in Romans 14:17, righteousness, peace, and joy in the Holy Spirit are characteristics of God's kingdom. When we live according to His direction, rather than indulging our own appetites, we experience life and peace (Rom. 8:6).

This makes one wonder whether rampant health issues and insecurity in modern society have something to do with lawlessness in our land. When everyone does their own thing, rather than what the Word of God defines as acceptable behavior, it's no wonder we don't experience inner or external peace! It's time to start living in ways the Lord considers righteous, so we can enjoy rest in our bodies, souls and spirits and avoid conflict in our homes, communities and nation.

Lord, You see the chaos in my body and my mind. What do I need to change to enjoy the effects of righteous conduct? Please help me live according to Your standards, so I experience Your peace. You see the turmoil in our society. Do the same for others in this nation, so we can dwell safely with nothing to make us afraid.

Day 42: God of War and Peace

*"I form the light, and create darkness.
I make **peace**, and create calamity.
I am Yahweh, who does all
these things."* (Isaiah 45:7)

This verse is part of a prophecy regarding a man not yet born, written about 100 years before its fulfillment! Beginning with Isaiah 44:28 through 45:13, the Lord disclosed His plan to use the pagan King Cyrus to bring His exiled people back to their own land in peace.

The entire passage emphasizes the sovereignty of Yahweh over all He created. In Isaiah 45:1-3, the Lord talked about how He would empower Cyrus to conquer the ancient Middle East, subduing nations before him, opening doors, making rough places smooth, and giving him hidden treasures. For the sake of His chosen people, God gave this Persian his title, without the man even knowing Yahweh personally (v. 4)!

In verses 5-6, the Lord asserted His uniqueness and superiority over other so-called gods. Then Yahweh described His ability to control nature (vv. 7-8).

Considering the magnitude and scope of our Creator's power, Isaiah wondered why anyone would argue with Yahweh about what He chooses to do. Verse 9 says, *"Woe to him who strives with his Maker...!"* Since the Lord made earth and all who inhabit it, He has every right to do as He pleases—including raising up a foreigner to release the exiles of Israel and authorize them to rebuild the holy city, Jerusalem (vv. 11-13).

Many Christians today are reluctant to imagine that God could be responsible for things we might classify as "bad," including war and catastrophic events. Yet this chapter tells us He forms both light and darkness. He makes peace and brings about calamity.

As Romans 8:28 says, the Lord ultimately works everything out for our well-being, just as He did for Israel. Yet His actions may not always make sense at the time. We need to trust that our Creator knows what He's doing.

Lord, I acknowledge Your right to rule over what You have made. Help me rest in Your sovereign care and not complain when You do something unexpected.

Day 43: Peace for the Righteous

*"Oh that you had listened to my commandments! Then your **peace** would have been like a river, and your righteousness like the waves of the sea.*

*"There is no **peace"**, says Yahweh, "for the wicked."* (Isaiah 48:18 & 22)

This passage comes from a chapter where God addressed those who claimed to know Him, but didn't live like it. In verse one, He said, *"...You swear by Yahweh's name, and make mention of the God of Israel, but not in truth, nor in righteousness."*

The children of Israel were so obstinate, God said, *"your neck is an iron sinew, and your brow brass"* (v. 4). If His prophetic words had not been recorded far in advance, the people would've credited their idols with what occurred (vv. 3 & 5-7)! It was a good thing the Lord was so patient with them (vv. 8-9). Through the fulfillment of His promised judgments, He refined them *"in the furnace of affliction"* (vv. 10-11).

Our God wants to bless, not discipline. He reminded Israel He existed before the world began and formed the earth and the heavens

(vv. 12-13). By His power He would raise up someone to overturn their Chaldean oppressors (vv. 14-15). He'd lead the Israelites safely back to their homeland from Babylon, just as He had brought them to the Promised Land from Egypt (vv. 20-21).

Calling Himself *"the Holy One of Israel,"* Yahweh said He'd teach His people to profit and lead them in the way they should go (vv. 16-17). In verse 18, God revealed that the secret to prosperous, healthy, happy living is to do what He says. In contrast, if you won't obey, don't expect good things to happen (v. 22)!

Do you long for peace like a river? How are you living? Are you listening to God and doing what He says, or picking and choosing what commands to obey? The only channel of peace is knowing and following the One True God.

Lord, You are the One who teaches us to profit. I submit. Help me follow Your commandments, so I can enjoy never-ending peace.

Day 44: Messengers of Peace

How beautiful on the mountains
are the feet of him who brings
good news, who publishes **peace**,
...who proclaims salvation, who says to Zion,
"Your God reigns!" (Isaiah 52:7)

In Isaiah 52, the Lord expressed His love
for Israel. Personifying Zion, a poetic name for
Jerusalem, Yahweh urged the holy city to put
on splendid robes, because she would no longer
be violated by those who were not set apart to
the Lord (v. 1). She was released from captivity
(v. 2).

God hinted at our salvation through Jesus'
blood when He said, *"You were sold for noth-*
ing; and you will be redeemed without money"
(v. 3). The Lord was indignant that those who
ruled over His exiled people mocked and ma-
ligned His reputation (v. 5). In verse six He
said something along the lines of "I'll show
them!" But His concern was that His own people would know His name—referring to God's
character.

That's where this verse about bringing good
news comes in. Feet are not generally very
pretty. Not many would say to their lover, "You
have the most beautiful feet!" Feet are usually

dirty, calloused and ugly—if they are visible at all. But God says feet that transport the bearer of good news about His reign and the peace that comes from it are beautiful.

Verses 8-9 talk about watchmen (a euphemism for prophets) and desolate places in Jerusalem breaking out in song, because Yahweh would comfort and redeem His people when He returned to their holy city. He planned to roll up His sleeves and save Israel in front of all the nations (v. 10). Not only that, but *"all the ends of the earth"* have the opportunity to see *Yeshua Elohim*—Jesus, the salvation of God.

Do you have beautiful feet? Are you telling others the good news regarding the peace that comes from knowing God and being ransomed from slavery to sin by Jesus' blood?

Lord, thank You for taking it upon Yourself to redeem us. Give me "beautiful feet" that carry me to those who need to hear the gospel.

Day 45: Our Penalty for His Peace

But he was pierced for our transgressions.
He was crushed for our iniquities.
The punishment that brought our **peace**
was on him; and by his wounds we are healed.
(Isaiah 53:5)

Isaiah 52:13-53:12 describes what Derek Prince called "The Divine Exchange." In a sermon and booklet by that name, he summed up the crucifixion this way: "[T]he evil due to us came upon Jesus, that, in return, the good due to Jesus might be offered to us."[1]

Christ was the Servant of Yahweh who conducted Himself wisely (Isa. 52:13). Nevertheless, He was beaten beyond recognition (v. 14). There was nothing in His appearance that drew people to Him (Isa. 53:2). *"He was despised, and rejected by men..."* (v. 3).

His contemporaries thought the Lord deserved the punishment He received. Yet our sins caused Him to be beaten, bruised, pierced and slain. He was disciplined so we could be reconciled with God. Jesus took the blows that purchased our healing from the diseases,

---

[1] Prince, Derek. *The Divine Exchange*. Derek Prince Ministries—International, 1995. pp. 8-9.

sorrows, griefs and pains He bore in our behalf (vv. 3-5).

Every human being is like a sheep that has wandered from the flock, going our own ways, but Yahweh put the consequences for our wrongdoings onto the Good Shepherd (v. 6). Although He never did anything dishonest, Jesus didn't utter a word in His own defense (v. 7). He was treated unjustly, like a common criminal, by those who carried out His sentence (vv. 8-9).

All this was for our benefit. The Lord caused this suffering, so Jesus would be an offering to make us right in God's sight (vv. 10-11). Thankfully, He'll be abundantly compensated for all He did to take our place and gain Yahweh's favor toward us (vv. 11-12).

Have you received the riches of heaven secured at Jesus' expense? If not, thank Him now for what He did and ask for that forgiveness, favor and restoration He offers.

Lord, thank You for taking the punishment I deserved at the cross. Please grant me peace and wholeness in exchange for my sins.

Day 46: Peace We Can Count On

*"For the mountains may depart,
and the hills be removed; but my loving
kindness will not depart from you, and my
covenant of **peace** will not be removed,"
says Yahweh who has mercy on you.*

*All your children will be taught by Yahweh;
and your children's **peace** will be great.*
(Isaiah 54:10 & 13)

Many people steer clear of prophetic books in the Old Testament, because they contain "hard words" of correction. Yet they miss out on beautiful messages of love and assurance found within passages such as this.

Having expressed His anger with unfaithful Israel—even symbolically divorcing the nation (Isa. 50:1)—the Lord was ready to proclaim good news. After revealing the atonement provided through His "suffering Servant," Yahweh comforted Israel, speaking as if the nation was a woman rejected by her husband.

Those who have experienced the pain of widowhood or divorce can relate to this passage. We long for assurance that we will not be left alone again. Yahweh not only declared, *"your Maker is your husband,"* but He promised to make up for the grief He had caused while disciplining His wayward bride (Isa. 54:4-8).

Rather than relying on imperfect parents, priests and prophets to educate the generations to come, the Lord said He Himself would train them in righteousness, so they could enjoy blessings instead of curses and well-being instead of trouble (v. 13).

Not everyone loves the people of God, so He promised to keep them safe, regardless of how many nations tried to attack. In verse 17 He said: *"No weapon that is formed against you will prevail; and you will condemn every tongue that rises against you in judgment. This is the heritage of Yahweh's servants...."*

Are you feeling forsaken, unloved and insecure? God's love is unfailing. His presence and protection guarantee our peace. Worried about your children? Entrust them to the Lord. He's the best teacher.

Lord, thank You for caring for me and those I love. Teach us to walk in Your ways, so we can enjoy the security of a right relationship with You.

Day 47: Joy and Peace for All Creation

For you shall go out with joy,
*and be led out with **peace**.*
The mountains and the hills will
break out before you into singing;
and all the trees of the fields
will clap their hands. (Isaiah 55:12)

Can you imagine mountains singing or trees clapping? What a sight! This verse reminds me of Jesus' words on Palm Sunday. When ordered by the Pharisees to rebuke His disciples, He replied, *"I tell you that if these keep silent, the stones will cry out!"* (Luke 19:40, LEB).

In Isaiah 55:1-2, the Lord invited people to acquire true food and drink for free, rather than wasting resources on what cannot satisfy. He urged, *"Seek Yahweh while he may be found. Call on him while he is near,"* promising an *"everlasting covenant"* with whomever would listen (vv. 3 & 6).

To experience true peace, we need God's mercy and pardon; we must forsake wicked thoughts and actions and return to Him (v. 7). We may think people ought to earn God's favor, but Yahweh said His thoughts and ways are different and far superior than ours (vv. 8-9).

His power is greater, too. As precipitation causes plants to grow for food, so God's Word contains the ability to accomplish whatever mission He intended for it (vv. 10-11). He's going to redeem humanity, and when He does, celebration on a grand scale is inevitable!

Romans 8:22 says, *"...all creation has been groaning with the pains of childbirth up to the present time"* (GW). But Jesus has reversed the curse against mankind and creation. Someday evergreens will replace thorns, and God's goodness will be remembered forever (Isa. 55:13).

Have you turned from vain pursuits, ideas and actions to enjoy God's favor and blessing? Don't leave it to rocks and trees to praise Him. Clap your hands, raise your voice, and let Him know how happy you are!

Heavenly Father, I acknowledge that Your ideas and ways are far better than I can imagine. Thank you for all You have done and are doing to restore peace to my life and everything You created.

Day 48: Removed from Calamity

The righteous perish,
and no one lays it to heart.
Merciful men are taken away,
and no one considers that
the righteous is taken away from the evil.
*He enters into **peace**....* (Isaiah 57:1-2)

Have you ever considered that, rather than being punishment, an unexpected death may actually be a tremendous blessing—a way for God to remove faithful individuals from further harm? That's what this passage is about.

Previously, in Isaiah 53, we saw how people thought Jesus was being punished for His own sins when He was crucified. I'm sure folks gossiped about Stephen and others who were martyred for their faith. Yet Jesus said persecution is a sure sign we are doing something right, even though it may not seem that way (Mat. 5:10-12).

The Lord warned that some people who love and serve Him would face persecution and even death; yet He promised His presence through suffering and rewards thereafter (Rev. 2:9-10). Others, He said He would keep, or preserve, *"from the hour of testing, which is to come on the whole world..."* (Rev. 3:10).

In Isaiah 57:15, Yahweh called Himself, *"the One who is high and lifted up, who inhabits eternity,"* who dwells *"in the high and holy place, and also with him who is of a contrite and lowly spirit..."* (ESV). Things may be rough for a while, but God's heart is to restore peace to those who wander from Him and to those who remain faithful (vv. 16-18).

If you're missing someone precious who seemed to be snatched away by death too soon, let this be a comfort to you: According to Psalms 116:15, God considers the death of His saints as precious/costly/highly valued. He doesn't take it lightly, because He's aware of the cost to you. Nevertheless, sometimes His plan is to do it as a favor to that individual.

Lord Jesus, You are fully acquainted with the pain we feel at the loss of a loved one. Comfort our hearts. Help us to celebrate our dear one's rest in Your presence and allow You to do Your good work in us.

Day 49: Paths That Don't Lead to Peace

*They don't know the way of **peace**;*
and there is no justice in their ways.
They have made crooked paths for themselves;
*whoever goes in them doesn't know **peace**.*
(Isaiah 59:8)

Isaiah 59 addresses people steeped in sin, who complain about negative circumstances. In verses 1-2, Yahweh said it's not His fault they're in trouble. He's fully capable of helping them, but their sin has separated them from God, so He doesn't listen or pay attention to their cries. Verses 5-7 talk about all the hurtful things they've said and done that have brought violence and destruction wherever they go.

It makes no sense to expect peace and tranquility while all you've done is evil. Don't expect a favorable destination when you keep following twisted paths! As the Apostle Paul wrote in Galatians 6:7-8, we reap what we sow: *"If you plant in the soil of your corrupt nature, you will harvest destruction..."* (GW).

You can't expect justice and righteousness to be given to you when you're not dispensing it to others. You can't expect revelation when you surround yourself with darkness. And you can't expect God to save you, when you lie, oppress

others and incite rebellion against the Lord.
(vv. 9-15)

In the absence of someone to bridge the barrier between God and man, Yahweh took it upon Himself to set things right; Jesus brought us salvation (v. 16). Those who refuse to submit will face God's judgment (vv. 17-18). Yet Yahweh promised, *"A Redeemer will come to Zion, and to those who turn from disobedience in Jacob..."* (v. 20).

To those who fear Him, He will reveal His glory and grant His Word and His Spirt (vv. 19 & 21). As Paul said in Romans 8:6, *"For the mindset of the flesh is death, but the mindset of the Spirit is life and peace"* (LEB).

Lord, I realize my attitudes and speech are not what they should be. I've listened to bad advice and gone down the wrong paths. Please redirect me. Help me follow Your Spirit so I can enjoy harmonious living with You and others.

Day 50: Ever-Flowing Peace

*For Yahweh says, "Behold, I will extend **peace** to her like a river, and the glory of the nations like an overflowing stream...."* (Isaiah 66:12)

In Isaiah 66:7-14, the Lord depicted the faithful of Israel—symbolically called by the name of the nation's capital, Zion, or Jerusalem—as a woman's children. In verse 8, Yahweh asked, *"Shall a land be born in one day? Shall a nation be born at once? For as soon as Zion travailed, she gave birth to her children."* The rebirth of the nation of Israel was sudden, with God Himself bringing about its successful delivery (v. 9).

Those who love the city of God are invited to rejoice with Jerusalem, just as family and friends celebrate with the mother of a newborn baby (v. 10a). Those who've mourned over her desolation can anticipate the comfort and glory God abundantly provides Jerusalem (vv. 10b-11).

The imagery in verses 12-13 is so rich: Not only does God promise a continuous stream of peace and safety to Jerusalem, but prosperity, as well. The glory, honor and abundant riches of the nations are described as a stream overflowing its banks. His sustenance and nurture is compared to what a mama gives her nursing infant. The comfort He gives His beloved is like the tenderness a mother shows her child! Verse 14 foretells emotional and physical healing, as well.

Do you see all the elements of *shalom*? Herein is contentment, favor, happiness, health, peace, prosperity, quiet, rest, safety, tranquility, welfare and well-being. Whatever a soul desires is found where godly worship is restored!

Do you long for the restoration of Israel— not only as a sovereign nation acknowledged and enriched by the world, but also as a center for worship of the One True God? Psalms 122:6 says those who love and pray for the peace of Jerusalem will prosper. When we love the nation God loves, we share in her blessings!

Lord, we love Your nation and Your people. We pray that You draw them in and let us share in the blessings in store for Your dear children.

Day 51: False Comfort

*"They have healed also the hurt of my people superficially, saying, **'Peace, peace!'** when there is no **peace**."* (Jeremiah 6:14)

One definition of *shalom* is wholeness or health. That's also a component of *yeshuah*, the Hebrew word for salvation, from which we get the names Joshua and Jesus. As we saw in Isaiah 53, Christ's suffering not only made it possible for us to be forgiven from sin and reconciled to God, but it also secured our healing.

However, people won't accept a gift they don't believe is available or desirable. That's why it's so important to make people aware of their sin and its consequences first, and then tell them about the free gift of salvation. A great example of this bad news to good news approach is found in Romans 6:23.

What Jeremiah exposed in this and other prophecies was how God's people were being lied to by false prophets who wanted them to feel good about themselves, rather than confronting their sins. They were like some doctors—giving people a drug to dull their pain, but not treating its underlying cause.

Regarding these false prophets, the Lord said, *"They say continually to those who despise me, 'Yahweh has said, "You will have **peace**;"' and to everyone who walks in the stubbornness of his own heart they say, 'No evil will come on you'"* (Jer. 23:17). They lulled the wicked into a false sense of security, keeping them from admitting their sin and their need for a change of heart. Thus, they were also robbed of the salvation, protection and restoration the Lord grants those who repent and turn to Him.

Are you giving people false peace, telling them everything will be okay, when they have not aligned themselves with God's conditions for *shalom*? Level with them, *"speaking the truth in love"* (Eph. 4:15), so they can receive true healing and peace with God.

Father, forgive me for offering false comfort to others instead of being honest about their situations. Grant me the love and courage to confront their sins and point them to the Source of peace.

Day 52: Peace in Exile

*"Seek the **peace** of the city where I have caused you to be carried away captive, and pray to Yahweh for it; for in its **peace** you will have **peace**."* (Jeremiah 29:7)

After the first wave of Jews were deported to Babylon, the Lord prompted Jeremiah the prophet to write to the exiles in that foreign land (Jer. 29:1-3). False prophets were giving the impression that their stay in Nebuchadnezzar's kingdom would be brief, despite the message Yahweh had already given that they would be there for 70 years (Jer. 25:11 & 29:8-10).

Yahweh's command was: *"Build houses and live in them; plant gardens and eat their produce"* (Jer. 29:5, ESV). He also encouraged them to marry and have kids so their population would grow (v. 6). God wanted the people to settle down, pray for their leaders and do what they could to make the most of their circumstances, until the appointed time of their sojourn was up and the Lord brought them back home.

In this day and age when there's so much violence and upheaval, many people have been displaced from their ancestral homes. Refugees abound, and many are living as strangers in a land that seems foreign to them. Even if you're still in the country of your origin, living in a different region can seem unfamiliar, if the culture and dialect are different than where you grew up.

Wherever we go, believers must resist the temptation to live as transients in survival mode. As the Lord guides and provides, we need to send down roots and build our families—to "bloom where we're planted," as the saying goes. We must get involved in the culture, politics and defense of the community, state and nation where we're living and try to make a difference there—for the sake of our own families and those around us. For, as that region prospers, so will we.

Heavenly Father, You put me here for a reason. Show me what that is. Help me seek the well-being of the community around me, so we can all enjoy Your blessings.

Day 53: God's Good Plans

*"For I know the thoughts that I think toward you," says Yahweh, "thoughts of **peace**, and not of evil, to give you hope and a future."*
(Jeremiah 29:11)

This verse comes from the letter Jeremiah wrote to Jewish exiles in Babylon. To these people who felt hated by Yahweh, because He had sent them far from home, God offered reassurance of His love and concern for them. He'd prophesied calamity against the Jews because of their rebellion against Him, yet His intentions were actually good. Although times were rough, they would eventually get better, but Judah needed to rethink their ideas about Yahweh first.

To those who felt as far from God as they were from their beautiful temple in Jerusalem, the Lord said, *"You shall call on me, and you shall go and pray to me, and I will listen to you. You shall seek me, and find me, when you search for me with all your heart."* (Jer. 29:12-13). Up until that point, the people had worshiped Yahweh *and* idols. They consulted Him, but were listening to false prophets who said what they wanted to hear.

They needed to come to a point of desperation where they would not be satisfied by anything but the Word of the Lord. Then He would be found by them and would gather them all up from the places where they had been scattered to bring His faithful ones home (v. 14).

Are you feeling far from God? Does it seem like your life is full of nothing but trouble and your prayers just ricochet off the walls? Maybe it's because your heart isn't 100% convinced that God loves you and wants the best for you. Perhaps you don't really love and trust the Lord with your whole being. He really wants to give you a future filled with hope and peace, but it starts with you seeking God and His will alone.

Father, forgive me for doubting Your good intentions for me. Help me to seek You first, so that all the other things I need will fall into place.

Day 54: Restoring Health and Well-being

*"'...I will cure them; and I will reveal to them abundance of **peace** and truth.*

*This city will be to me for a name of joy, for praise, and for glory, before all the nations of the earth, which will hear all the good that I do to them, and will fear and tremble for all the good and for all the **peace** that I provide to it.'"* (Jeremiah 33:6 & 9)

God isn't a show-off. Nevertheless, He loves to demonstrate what He can do. He loves to delight His own, because their pleasure brings Him pleasure.

At the beginning of this chapter, Yahweh told Jeremiah, *"Call to me, and I will answer you. I will tell you great and mysterious things that you do not know"* (Jer. 33:3, GW). Even while He was allowing the destruction of Jerusalem by Nebuchadnezzar, God was planning for Judah's restoration. He was eager to tell His prophet the secrets of how He would re-establish the nation and its capital, and how He would revive His people and bring glory to His name because of it!

Health in body and soul are part of the completeness and wholeness *shalom* brings. When

God's people are well off, others see it and want to know why. In Israel's case, it was because of the Lord's eternal covenant with them through Abraham, Isaac and Jacob. In the case of Christians, we enjoy *shalom* because of the new covenant God makes with us through the blood of Jesus Christ.

When God does good things for His own, it results in praise and glory for Him. In 2 Corinthians 9:8-15, we see that God's generosity to us allows us to bless others, who in turn bless God.

Lord, You are a gracious God who loves to bless us so that we can bring blessing to You and others. Heal my body, soul and spirit. Open my heart to receive what You want to give; open my hands to give what You want me to share, and open my mouth to give You the thanksgiving, praise and glory You deserve.

Day 55: Safe Pasture

*"'I will make with them a covenant of **peace**,
and will cause evil animals to cease
out of the land. They will dwell securely
in the wilderness, and sleep in the woods.'"*
(Ezekiel 34:25)

In Ezekiel 34, Yahweh described the people of Israel as sheep and their leaders as shepherds. He expressed extreme displeasure with unrighteous shepherds who fed themselves while neglecting His flock (vv. 1-3). His people were going astray, being devoured by predators, and getting sick or injured with no one to care for them (vv. 4-6). Since the shepherds of Israel were killing the sheep or treating those that weren't lost harshly, God said He would remove them (vv. 7-10).

In contrast, the Lord promised to go looking for the lost sheep, rescue them, gather them up and lead them to good places to graze and rest (vv. 11-15). Yahweh said He would bind up the injured and strengthen the weak (v. 16). He planned to judge between individual sheep and get rid of the bullies among them (vv. 17-22).

Then He'd appoint David as a good shepherd to rule over them instead (vv. 23-24). Under this benevolent administration, both the people and the land would be productive and without reproach (vv. 25-31).

In John 10, Jesus described Himself as our Good Shepherd. He frequently felt compassion on the crowds, because they were *"like sheep without a shepherd"* (Mat. 9:36 & Mar. 6:34). In Luke 19:10, He said He *"came to seek and to save that which was lost."*

Jesus was the One through whom God established His covenant of *shalom* by which everyone who believes in Christ receives good guidance, safety and security. Wherever we happen to go, He watches over us and cares for our every need. Nothing and no one can harm His own.

Lord, You are a Good Shepherd. I can trust You to look after me. Help me follow You and stay away from so-called "shepherds" who mistreat, neglect or exploit others. Remove them from power and give Your people leaders like Jesus, instead, so Your flock can dwell in safety.

Day 56: Peace Where God Is Present

*Moreover I will make a covenant of **peace** with them. It will be an everlasting covenant with them. I will place them, multiply them, and will set my sanctuary among them forever more. ...I will be their God, and they will be my people. The nations will know that I am Yahweh who sanctifies Israel, when my sanctuary is among them forever more.* (Ezekiel 37:26-28)

When God first made a covenant with His people in the wilderness, He gave them guidelines to live holy lives—even telling them how to dispose of waste and quarantine "unclean" individuals, because He dwelt among them in the camp (Num. 5:2-3 & Deu. 23:12-14). When the temple was built, there were guidelines for who could enter, when and how, because God occupied that, as well. After His people violated these guidelines, making themselves and their land unholy, Yahweh withdrew (Eze. 8-10).

Yet, the Lord promised to remedy this situation. In Daniel 9:24, He prophesied that the Messiah would come *"...to put an end to sin, and to atone for iniquity, to bring in everlasting righteousness..."* for the people of Israel and their holy city, Jerusalem (ESV). Within the seventy sets of seven years referred to in the prophecy, Jesus came and—in one day— paid the penalty for the sins of Israel, setting them apart and making them holy once again.

By the blood He shed at the cross, Jesus not only cleansed the Jews, but people of every other nation. In Isaiah 52:15, God said His suffering Servant would *"sprinkle many nations,"* thus purifying them from sin (LEB).

In John 14:23, Jesus said He and the Heavenly Father would come make their home in any individual who loves Him and keeps His commandments. In 1 Corinthians 6:19, the Apostle Paul wrote that believers are actually temples of the Holy Spirit. God doesn't just live *with* us, but *in* us under this everlasting covenant of peace!

Lord, thank You for cleansing us from sin and making Your home in those who believe in Jesus. Help me live a holy life, constantly enjoying your company.

Day 57: Peace That Strengthens

He said, "Greatly beloved man,
*don't be afraid. **Peace** be to you. Be strong.*
Yes, be strong." When he spoke to me,
I was strengthened.... (Daniel 10:19)

Have you ever noticed that paintings of Jesus often portray Him as anemic-looking and pale? It's always bothered me, because before becoming a rabbi, Jesus was a carpenter—no doubt carrying heavy blocks of wood. While the New Testament doesn't tell us what Christ looked like walking about Judea, we do have spectacular descriptions of His appearance before and after the incarnation.

In the tenth chapter of the book that bears his name, Daniel fasted and prayed three weeks, seeking revelation about a vision he'd received. In response to that prayer, the Lord Himself came to explain it.

Daniel 10:6 describes the "man" the prophet saw:

His body resembled yellow jasper, and his face had an appearance like light-ning. His eyes were like blazing torches; his arms and feet had the gleam of polished bronze. His voice

*thundered forth like the sound of a
large crowd"* (NET).

This sounds a lot like the description of the resurrected Christ in Revelation 1:9-17.

The air must've been charged with power, since the men accompanying Daniel trembled in terror, then ran and hid themselves—even though they couldn't see what he did (v. 7)! Daniel was so overwhelmed with physical and emotional exhaustion that twice the Lord had to touch him to strengthen the prophet. He urged Daniel not to be afraid but to be strong and courageous.

Once Daniel felt better, he was able to receive God's message. The glorious Savior told the prophet how precious he was in God's sight and how effective his prayers had been.

God doesn't want us to remain for long in dread and insecurity; He desires that we experience His peace. With Christ's reassuring words and restorative touch, we can regain our sense of well-being.

*Lord, thank You for the peace that comes
from Your throne to those who need it. Please
let me hear Your encouraging words and feel
Your tender touch whenever I'm uncertain
about the future.*

Day 58: Where Peace Dwells

*"'The latter glory of this house will be greater than the former...and in this place I will give **peace**,' says Yahweh of Armies."* (Haggai 2:9)

This prophecy concerning the second temple in Jerusalem was given to the Israelites who returned to rebuild the house of worship after seventy years of exile in Babylon. According to Ezra 3:10-13, old-timers present when the foundation was laid for the new temple wept as they compared it to the magnificent palace they remembered from before.

In Haggai 2:3, the Lord asked them, *"Who is left among you who saw this house in its former glory? How do you see it now? Isn't it in your eyes as nothing?"*

These men looked at the dimensions and materials of the building and were disappointed that it lacked the royal splendor a temple of Yahweh should have. Yet the Lord looked ahead to the time that place would be graced by the presence of His Anointed One. The very Son of God would enter this humble temple and preach peace to the people of Israel. Not only that, but by His sacrifice for sins, the long-awaited Messiah would eliminate the barrier between God and men, as signified by the tearing of the temple veil when Christ was crucified (Mar. 15:38).

When Jesus rose from the grave and ascended into heaven, something even more glorious happened. Not only were we granted peace with God through faith in Him, but He sent His Holy Spirit to occupy each believer and make *us* God's temples (1 Cor. 3:16). Together with believing Hebrews, Gentile Christians are built into a holy habitation for the Lord (Eph. 2:19-22).

According to Revelation 21:22, the greatest temple of all will exist on earth when the Father and Son come to live among men! Peace isn't tied to a place, but a Person.

Lord Jesus, You are indeed our peace, who came to unify all men in worship of the Father through the Son. Help me approach You daily in the temple of my heart and experience the peace You procured through Your sacrifice.

Day 59: Justice, Truth and Peace

"...speak every man the truth with
his neighbor. Execute the judgment of truth
*and **peace** in your gates, and let none of you*
devise evil in your hearts against his neighbor,
and love no false oath: for all these are things
that I hate," says Yahweh. (Zechariah 8:16-17)

Authenticity and integrity are important ingredients in a just and equitable society. For individuals to trust one another, for vulnerable members of a community to feel safe, there must be a climate of openness with mutual acceptance of and adherence to a high standard of righteousness. When deception, exploitation and abuse are tolerated, no one is at peace; we're constantly worried about someone taking advantage of us.

Zechariah 8 revealed what citizens of God's kingdom have to look forward to under His righteous reign: Jerusalem will be a "City of Truth," where men and women grow old and children play safely (vv. 3-5).

In verse 10, we read:

For before those days there was no
wages for man...neither was there any
peace to him who went out or came in,

because of the adversary. For I set all
men everyone against his neighbor.

There's no peace where everyone is looking out for their own interests, unconcerned about what's right or how their decisions will affect others.

Whereas rebellious, self-willed Israel was a curse among the nations, the Lord promised to make them a blessing instead (v. 13).

*For there shall be a sowing of **peace**.*
The vine shall give its fruit, and the
ground shall give its produce, and the
heavens shall give their dew. And I will
cause the remnant of this people to pos-
sess all these things. (Zec. 8:12, ESV,
emphasis added).

Revelation 21-22 describes the New Jerusalem where God's reign will be established on earth and evil will be expelled. Meanwhile, we plant seeds of peace by speaking the truth and loving others as ourselves, as Jesus taught.

Father, thank You for the peace and safety
coming soon. Help me bring peace to my
sphere of influence by speaking truth and
desiring what's best for my neighbors.

Day 60: Peaceable Kingdom

Rejoice greatly, daughter of Zion!
Shout, daughter of Jerusalem!
Behold, your King comes to you!
He is righteous, and having salvation;
lowly, and riding on a donkey,
even on a colt, the foal of a donkey.
...and he will speak **peace** *to the nations:*
and his dominion will be from sea to sea,
and from the River to the ends of the earth.
(Zechariah 9:9-10)

Matthew 21:1-9 and John 12:12-16 tell us this prophecy was fulfilled with Christ's triumphant entry into Jerusalem. The people welcomed their King by spreading coats and palm branches on the road, shouting, *"Hosanna! Blessed is he who comes in the name of the Lord!"* (Mar. 11:8-10).

Hosanna comes from two Hebrew words that mean "save now!" They're found in Psalms 118:25-26, which the people quoted as they met the Lord on the road. They thought Jesus was coming to save them from the Romans. But, as Psalms 118:27 indicated, first He had to come as a sacrifice to save them from their sins.

Because He was righteous—without fault of any kind—*"God made the one who did not know sin to be sin for us, so that in him we would become the righteousness of God"* (2 Cor. 5:21, NET).

As Zechariah foretold in our scripture for today, Jesus came amicably first: not riding a war horse but a donkey colt. He came to bring peace—initially to the Jews, then to *all* nations, even *"to the ends of the earth."* Those who submit to His Lordship have reason to rejoice, because He enables us to enjoy God's favor.

One day the King of Kings will come on a white horse to make war against those who deceive and enslave the world (Rev. 19:11-21). When the devil himself is defeated and everything that opposes God's righteous reign is removed, then peace will be established forever (Rev. 20-22)!

Thank You, Lord, that peace on earth is possible through the righteous reign of Jesus Christ. Remove from me anything that offends You, and make me an agent of Your kingdom, speaking shalom *to everyone I meet.*

Finding Peace with God

Believing that the only way for anyone to enjoy true peace is to align their hearts with King Jesus, I would be remiss if I failed to give those who have not yet embraced Him as their Lord and Savior the chance to do that.

In the Old Testament, Jesus was known as the "Prince of Peace." God gave us so many signs that pointed the way to Him. He fulfilled numerous prophecies about Messiah, the Anointed One the Jews were anticipating, including:

- His miraculous conception by a virgin (Isa. 7:14, Mat. 1:18-23, Luk. 1:30-35)

- His lineage through Abraham, Isaac, Jacob, Judah and David (Gen. 12:3, 17:19, 18:18, 21:12, 28:10-14 & 49:10; Jer. 23:5; Mat. 1:1-16; Luk. 3:23-38)

- His birthplace (Mic. 5:2, Mat. 2:1-6, Luk. 2:4-7)

- His family's sojourn in Egypt (Hos. 11:1, Mat. 2:14-15)

- His silence before false accusers, suffering in behalf of our sins and being executed with wrong-doers (Isa. 53, Mat.

26-27, Mar. 15:3-5 & 22-27, Luk. 23:32-33 & 40-43)

- The piercing of His body, offering of gall with vinegar, ridicule from the crowds, and guards gambling for His clothing (Psa. 22:14-18, 69:21, 109:25; Zec. 12:10; Mat. 27:33-44; Mar. 15:22-32; Luk. 23:33-39; Joh. 19:16-37)

- His death and resurrection after three days (Psa. 16:10, Hos. 6:2, Mat. 28:5-7, Mar. 16:1-7, Luk. 24:4-7, Act. 2:27-32).

Every human being is alienated from God, because we have failed to do what He says. That's called sin. Not one person can rightly claim they are good enough to escape punishment, because we have all broken God's Laws. (See Psalms 14:1-3 & 53:1-3, Romans 3:10-23, James 2:8-11, 1 John 1:8)

God loves every person and doesn't want any of us to be destroyed because of our sins. He wants all to enjoy peace and blessing, which is why He sent Jesus to die, so we can be restored to a right relationship with Him. He wants us to be saved by believing that truth. (2 Pet. 3:9, 1 Tim. 2:3-4, Joh. 3:16-18)

Jesus told His disciples He is the only way for us to get to God (Joh. 14:6). They, in turn, said salvation was found in no one else but

Him (Act. 4:11-12). The Apostle Paul said that peace with God comes through faith in the Lord Jesus Christ (Rom. 5:1). He died for the ungodly to save us from the punishment we deserved for our sins—reconciling the very people who had previously lived like enemies of God to Him (vv. 6-11).

To experience peace with God, here's what you need to do:

- **Admit you have done wrong and desire to do what's right.** Regarding anything that displeases the Lord, you should not only tell Him you are sorry and ask Him to forgive you for it, but also ask Him to take away the desire to do those things ever again (1 John 1:9).

- **Acknowledge your need for a Savior.** No one is able to save themselves; God has to do it for us by giving us faith in Jesus Christ (Eph. 2:8-9, Tit. 3:3-7).

- **Agree with God about Jesus.** Romans 10:9-11 & 13 says,

    If you declare that Jesus is Lord, and believe that God brought him back to life, you will be saved. By believing you receive God's approval, and by declaring

your faith you are saved. Scrip-
ture says, "Whoever believes in
him will not be ashamed."

So then, "Whoever calls on the
name of the Lord will be
saved." (GW)

- **Seek to be baptized in water and
  share your decision to follow Jesus
  with others.** The first sermon the
  Apostle Peter preached was that everyone should *"Repent and be baptized*
  [submerged in water] *in the name of
  Jesus Christ for the forgiveness of your
  sins..."* (Act. 2:38, ESV). Baptism is a
  way of identifying with the death and
  resurrection of Jesus, so everyone can
  see that we consider ourselves dead to
  sin but alive to God in Christ to do what
  honors Him (Rom. 6:3-14).

- **Ask the Holy Spirit to come live
  inside you and help you live at
  peace with God and others.** Jesus
  described the Holy Spirit as a Helper,
  Counselor and Teacher for those who do
  what He says (Joh. 14:15-26, 16:13-15).
  Only by following the Spirit can we
  please God; He lets us know we belong
  to God and makes us like Jesus (Rom.
  8).

126

If you have taken these steps to make peace with God today, please let me know! You can reach me through the contact page of my website at https://psalm8116.com/contact/. While you are there, you may enjoy exploring the content of that Bible-based website, which contains resources that can help you in your new relationship with God.

About the Author

Deborah Schaulis first gave her life to Christ when she was in elementary school and was baptized in water a couple years later. Yet, she didn't quite feel at peace with God until filled with the Holy Spirit as a teen and delivered from life-controlling issues in adulthood.

After two years of training in Youth With A Mission (YWAM), Deborah began to use her God-given gifts and talents to "creatively communicate God's truth for changed lives." Since then, she's been active in ministry at various churches, mission organizations, non-profit and business settings, sharing the love of Christ with whomever the Lord puts into her path. She loves teaching others how to study the Bible, hear God's voice, pray, exercise spiritual gifts, write and create.

Deborah's poetry, articles, short stories, essays, guest editorials and other works have been published in various magazines, newspapers, newsletters and anthologies. She has also edited several fiction and non-fiction works. The website *Honey from the Rock* at https://psalm8116.com features her commentary, resources and blogs about the Bible, as well as links to order her other books.

When not writing or volunteering, Deborah loves reading, hiking, photography and making various arts and crafts. She also thoroughly enjoys spending time with her husband, son, daughter-in-love, grandchildren and "grand-dog."

www.ingramcontent.com/pod-product-compliance
Lightning Source LLC
Chambersburg PA
CBHW011230120626
46549CB00008B/3208

* 9 7 9 8 9 9 0 2 4 6 1 9 5 *